THE 100

Greatest Ideas for
Building your Career

Ken Langdon

CAPSTONE

First published 2000 by
Capstone Publishing Limited
Oxford Centre for Innovation
Mill Street
Oxford OX2 0JX
United Kingdom
http://www.capstone.co.uk

British Library Cataloguing in Publication Data
A CIP catalogue record for this book is available from the British Library

ISBN 1-84112-101-0

Typeset in 11/14 pt Plantin by
Sparks Computer Solutions Ltd, Oxford
http://www.sparks.co.uk
Printed and bound by
T.J. International Ltd, Padstow, Cornwall

This book is printed on acid-free paper

Substantial discounts on bulk quantities of Capstone books are available to corporations, professional associations and other organisations. For details telephone Capstone Publishing on (+44-1865-798623) or fax (+44-1865-240941).

Contents

Seven Greatest Ideas for Getting a New Job   39

Eight Greatest Ideas for Standing Out in the Crowd   47

Four Greatest Ideas for Impressing the Management Panel

Seven Greatest Ideas for Leading a Team to Success   69

Four Greatest Ideas for Standing Out in the More Senior Crowd

Four Greatest Ideas for Spending the Organisation's Money Frugally

Six Greatest Ideas for Spending the Organisation's Money Cleverly

An Interlude

Six Greatest Ideas for Spending the Organisation's Money Lavishly

Eight Greatest Ideas for Things to Do Differently If You Are a Woman   119

Four Greatest Ways for Managing Projects   125

Six Greatest Ideas for Getting Nearer the Top   139

Ten Greatest Ideas for Winning at Office Politics   147

Three Greatest Ideas for Surviving Politics   155

Three Greatest Ideas for Enjoying the Last Rung   *157*

Acknowledgements

Richard Humphreys, chairman of more companies than I can remember, supplied many of the ideas in this book. He also read the first draft and suggested many improvements.

My daughter Kate organised the correspondence with the chairmen and CEOs that made it possible to quote their advice. She also did much of the library research.

I gratefully acknowledge their huge contributions.

Here is the number of employees at each level of a large aerospace company.

CEO	1
Divisional directors	10
General manager	20
Second line manager	100
First line manager	500
Supervisor	2500
Shop floor	37000

From this you can gather how sharp the pyramid of a large organisation is. The statistical chances of going from the shop floor to the very top are 39,999 to 1. Even if you make it to general manager, only 1 out of 31 people is going to make it all the way to CEO, and in getting to general manager you have defied odds of 8900 to 1.

So what distinguishes those who buck the odds and make it, and those who take longer than they hoped to get to a suitable level, or languish in a job which they feel does not stretch them enough, nor for that matter reward them enough?

Part of it is to do with skills and capabilities, or perhaps talent, but even the last of these can be developed and improved. Flair increases with the number of times you exercise it to take risks and think outside the square. But that is not all. If the best people, measured by strict logic, all got the jobs in front of other contenders, there would not be the degree of incompetence shown at most levels of industry and other organisations. There would not exist the politics and jealousies that are the mark of all large institutions.

Just think for a moment about how much of your career is left to chance. It depends on who happens to be your boss when you get promoted, for example, and who likes or dislikes him or her. It depends on the exigencies of the products and services you deliver and the markets you deliver them into. It depends on the economic climate and even who is in political control of the country. All of these are somewhat chancy. You have some control over how these elements come together, but certainly not all of them.

So what do you do when you are seeking to achieve a difficult business objective with a fair degree of uncertainty? Why, you make a plan, of course. You look at your strengths and weaknesses and develop a career strategy.

This book is about such a strategy and how others have found the key to different aspects of building careers. It does not, as do some human resource managers, pretend that the world is just, or that it owes you a living. Rather it takes on the world as it is. It looks at how you get as much control as you can over a world where 'life is mostly of froth and bubble'. When you look back on your career, which will the most descriptive quote be?

- *in the fell clutch of circumstance;*
- *I have not winced nor cried aloud;*
- *under the bludgeonings of chance;*
- *my head is bloody, but unbowed.*

Or do you learn from others and finish with a triumphant shout?

- *'tis not in mortals to command success,*
  But we'll do more, Sempronius; we'll deserve it.

Career clue from the boardroom

Take personal ownership for your personal and career development planning. Have a positive attitude and be prepared to adapt, change and exploit opportunities quickly and well.

John A. Hart (Group Personnel Director, PowerGen)

*E*ight *G*reatest *I*deas for *W*inning at *C*ompany *P*olitics

Introduction

It is not possible for any organisation to exist without some form of internal politics. The fact is that people disagree about the way ahead, and have different and often conflicting agendas and objectives. Face it; in company politics the competition is your colleagues. It is also very difficult to make a decision on behalf of an organisation without paying attention to what the implications of the decision are to you. Difficult and probably not desirable either, since business wants its people to achieve success and to be motivated to do it continuously. So, if company politics is going to permeate every decision that affects your career, we should start by looking at some brutal facts. After all, you need to do more than survive in this area. The Vicar of Bray played his organisation's politics well and survived, but he never made it to bishop. My Dad, watching the politics that my mother got into in a small local church was heard to murmur, 'The more I see of Christians, the more sorry I feel for the lions.' So, if the Church cannot avoid internal politics and strife, what chance has a profit-making body like a capitalist corporation?

This chapter is a series of warming-up exercises to get ready for the fray. Tell people what they need to know. *Communicate with your seniors in their terms Idea 2* helps you communicate with your boss. *Abolish your job Idea 6*, and *create a new post Idea 7* cover using your own efforts to alter the structure of the company. But we start with the most brutal truth of them all.

Idea 1 – Realise that you do not owe them anything

You have, nowadays particularly, to start from a rather cynical but practical viewpoint of your organisation. It is probably chaotic, either all the time or sometimes or in places. This is both a problem and an opportunity for the career-minded. Chaos means that, whatever it says about looking after you and your career, your company may very well not be able to carry it through. It is less able to do so now than it was in the past. During the nineties, for example, a huge number of trades and skills simply disappeared, replaced by the computer equivalent. Organisations have to take such technological change on board if they are to survive. In short, the organisation has to look after itself in a hard-nosed way, so you need to look after yourself.

The organisation is also not necessarily totally honest with its customers, nor with its suppliers and regulators, nor with its people. I do not say that it is not striving to be honest; I am merely pointing out that in a competitive and changing world an organisation will at some times be dishonest with everyone. How many times do we learn in the chairman's report that 'Our people are our greatest asset', and elsewhere in the annual report that the merger of one company into another resulted in a significant number of job savings?

And circumstances change. A promise made to a member of staff in good faith may become impracticable overnight. In this environment the safest view to take on your organisation is that you owe it your loyal support only as long as your objectives and the organisation's can coexist. So, it is more a question of jobs now than careers. Companies do not offer jobs for life and most successful careerists will change employers from time to time. Keep an open mind and don't get so set in your ways that you get caught out by a reorganisation in which you find yourself with the post 'co-ordinator of long-term planning'. Such a post almost certainly means that you are no longer part of those long-term plans.

This idea does not in any way advise you to be dishonest yourself. Indeed the careerist does well to heed the advice of Robert Townsend, at one time the CEO of Avis:

Except in poker, bridge and similar play period activities, don't con anybody. Not your spouse, not your children, not your employees, not your customers, not your stockholders, not your boss, not your associates, not your suppliers, not your regulatory authorities, not even your competitors.

This was written some time ago and still holds true, but most career players will tell you that business life has, in some circumstances, moved into the Townsend's 'similar play periods' of poker and bridge. The company man is extinct; the new watchwords are fluidity of labour.

Career clue from the boardroom

Let us balance this idea with the four *C*s – a chairman's thoughts on making it to the top:

- Wherever you are, well honed *communication* skills are highly important.
- *Continued learning* – lifelong learning is no longer a buzz word but a real necessity to be conscientiously practised.
- *Confidence* in yourself – never be afraid to seize sensible opportunities – be ambitious.
- *Care* and attention to those you love and indeed to those you work with. A selfish narrow life soon becomes too difficult to correct.

Murray Stuart, CBE (Chairman, Scottish Power)

Idea 2 – Communicate with your seniors in their terms

High-profile people get noticed, and the higher up the people doing the noticing the better. Form a plan for having more than your fair share of senior management's attention, and then communicate well.

We shall see in many of the greatest ideas how important it is that your boss thinks you are brilliant, and that you help to make him or her look brilliant as well. Not only your boss, but also your boss's boss. Make sure you are aware of the issues that are taking up both of these people's time. Be prepared to *put up a paper* on the topic *Idea 48*, and it is in this regard that communicating with your boss falls into our first thoughts on company politics. Think through, for example, the level of detail your boss wants to read and hear. As you go up the organisation, you find people who are capable of going into detail, but less likely to want to or need to.

Career clue from the boardroom

Keep your executive summaries short and snappy. If you need to pass the weight test, put it in the appendices. That will keep the 'jobsworths' happy but won't detain the people you really want to notice your talents. Remember, you are trying to impress someone above you. He or she did not get where they are today by spending self-enhancement time on verbiage from a junior; some ambitious little swot's worthy but tedious *magnum opus*. By definition their time is in short supply; it is valuable to them. They have lunch to drink, golf to play and even more important people to impress. Actually, if they are not like that, you've got a problem. They will be no use to you and your career. If your boss is into detail treat him or her as a roadblock to your career and take avoiding action.

Richard Humphreys (Serial Chairman)

Theirs is the helicopter view that surveys the world from on high. In both written and oral communications, put your best efforts into clear, simple and short management summaries.

There are many ways of communicating with the great and the good in your organisation outside the normal business environment. Volunteer for these. I don't mean volunteer for anything that has a low impact, no matter how worthy. There is no point in being a member of the St John Ambulance team at the local football ground, worthy though that is, but there may be a point in being the fire officer for your floor. Check it out first; does it get you in front of the director of logistics, for example. More promising than these is representing the company at sport. If you are good at sport, senior managers will bask in your limelight. If you do it for fun, you will still be seen if the people you are trying to impress come to the golf match themselves or are invited to have dinner, make a witty speech, (opportunity to help with some gags here) and present the prizes.

Another good place to volunteer is the company newsletter, particularly if it involves interviewing senior people from time to time. Only speak at the Christmas party if you are really good at making people laugh. Do speak at conferences where being amusing is a significant but secondary requirement.

Idea 3 – Compromise, play the percentages

A lot of people fail to build their careers at the fastest speed possible because they find it difficult to compromise. You have to lose battles to win wars. Don't go to the wire to win a point against a colleague. Nobody likes the pedant who corrects the small detail. The big picture is the aiming point; don't get caught up in the minutiae. Don't make enemies unnecessarily. In the normal world of society it is a common saw that 'We must forgive, but not necessarily forget.' I find it the opposite in business. An enemy may very well have forgotten what you did to them, but they will never forgive you.

Take, for example, operational targets. Your boss in most circumstances wants you to achieve yours. He or she is not, therefore, going to push down on you more than they have to. But sometimes their task means that you will be given higher objectives than you think is possible. Don't whinge. Put up a paper explaining how you are going to try to achieve the target but where you see the problems. With a bit of luck your boss will see a way to help you to achieve the original target or see the logic behind your potential shortfall and change the objective. It is also a matter of timing. You, the 'can-do' person, in an environment where the boss is proposing a mission impossible will always wait for someone else to point this out to him or her. At all times avoid taking the negative view.

Career case in point

At the start of the company year, a sales manager was informing her sales people of their sales targets for the year. They were all challenging to say the least. One extreme reaction was a salesman who simply accepted his target with no complaint or even discussion. Another salesman went on and on moaning about how it was impossible; and that he should have less; and that his patch had difficulties that the others didn't; and so on.

Eventually the first salesman spoke his first words and offered to swap his target and patch for the other's. 'You take my sales territory and target and I'll take yours.' This was a tactic much more likely to lead to approval from the boss. The whinger was forced to climb down and lost face.

Idea 4 – Whose idea was it anyway?

This one is quite straightforward. Your boss must think that other people believe that your good ideas are his. You must make sure that other people know that both your good ideas and your boss's good ideas are really yours. Remember that 'Success has many parents, failure is an orphan.' One good idea often ends up in the 'Strengths' box of an awful lot of appraisals.

Idea 5 – Help the aged

The directors at the top of the organisation are, by definition, older than most of their subordinates. This gives them some disadvantages if some management techniques or technologies have been introduced when they were already at the top. They know nothing of them, and sometimes get into a position where this is a problem. I once walked into the office of such a director on the day when his first on-line terminal had been delivered on to his desk. 'There is something wrong with it,' he said, 'I've been fiddling about with it for hours. I have been through the start up procedure in the manual and still there is nothing on the screen. I'll have to get the computer people in tomorrow.' I happened to know that there was a brightness button at the back of the terminal; so I turned this up and the terminal sprang to life. 'It's pathetic,' I said, 'that should never have been left off when they delivered the terminal.'

I had done a lot for him in that moment. First I had put the blame for his incompetence firmly with someone else, important for him not to lose face with me. Secondly I had saved him from an embarrassing, though short, visit from the help desk, and thirdly I was in a position to show him round the system further and we spent a happy half-hour doing just that. But mainly I had put him a big step ahead of the other directors who probably did not know about the brightness button, and who certainly were unfamiliar with the rest of the system. I could imagine the scene

Career clue

When you are in a junior position piggy-back on the success of your immediate boss. Higher up you may have to piggyback on the demise of your immediate boss. Try to find some way of making your boss's boss look like a star.

the next day, as he modestly helped others to get started, and was congratulated by the chairman for getting to grips with this new-fangled stuff so quickly.

Idea 6 – Abolish your job

This may seem a risky thing to do, but it is a great mistake in career planning to assume that the current management structure is the one in which you have to succeed. Indeed the opposite is the case.

This profound observation has good reason behind it. Many jobs exist because they have always done so rather than because they represent the best way of doing things. If someone goes into the job and does things the right way, they are probably going outside the original job description that set the post up in the first place. This changed way of operating gets results, but when the person who made the change leaves, his or her boss will have to change the structure and job description so that the new post consolidates the new way of working. The lesson here is to use your influence and authority to get the best results possible without paying much attention to how things were done in the past.

Career clue from the boardroom

Henry Lewis was the CEO of Marks and Spencer. When asked why, out of all the management trainees that he joined with, he had made it right to the top said, 'You know, I really have no idea.' After some thought he added, 'But I have noticed that every job I have ever done has been abolished after I left it.'

Idea 7 – Create a new post

The corollary of abolish your job is also true. Managers who succeed are the ones who help the organisation keep up to date and who help to prevent it ossifying.

Career clue from the boardroom

A president of RCA is reported to have answered the question, 'Why, when so many were called were you chosen?' with the opposite of Henry Lewis's remark. He also purported not to know, but said, 'I have noticed that no job I ever did existed before I got it.'

It is easier to create a new job if the change will help the organisation achieve its objectives better, but it is possible to do it for your own purposes alone. Possibly starting from *putting up a paper Idea 48*, the creation of a new job is in two parts. First formulate the changed way of doing business that will ensure that the job will exist. Sell this first. That is, show what the changes will do in business terms rather than in structural or people terms. If you reveal your hand at this stage, there is a good chance that you are mistiming it by being too early. Don't give anyone the opportunity to say that what you are doing is for your own greater glory rather than the advancement of the organisation. Having sold the change, produce your implementation plan and, of course, include the new positions required. Do not at this stage play any kind of shrinking violet game; clearly show that you are the person for the role you have chosen and defined. You have the business benefits behind you and they have been agreed, so tell people that you should have the job. Make sure the new job description has all the elements needed for the next step – access to senior management and a high profile when required. The risk and return on this career procedure will be very good if you have got it right. After all, you have moulded a job where the circumstances and your skills will be a perfect fit.

Idea 8 – Make a splash in your new company

If you make a move to a new company, you are at some disadvantage against your fellow managers. They know the ropes and how to shine in the existing environment. It is therefore a very good idea to do something very early on in your new career to question that environment and change it in a high-profile way.

So, think about it when you are making a change of employer. Look at why the company has hired you. If you are coming in at a fairly high level it is likely that the people who hired you saw you as a change agent (*rule of 20% Idea 44*), for a part of their culture with which they are dissatisfied – new blood and all that.

Career case in point

A manager moved from a telecommunications company to another larger and longer established company. He knew, from his competitive knowledge and from things said at the interview, that senior management were implementing a huge change programme aimed at knocking the old-fashioned corners off their long-serving managers. These people were accustomed to a hierarchical rather deferential culture where seniority counted highly. They were also struggling with the concept that the customer was king. The first thing the new boy did on his first day was to remove every car parking space allocated on the basis of management seniority. He re-allocated the best spaces to customers only.

Also in his tour of the car park, he realised that there were some areas that were not only dark but also outside the range of the security cameras. Accordingly, he allocated the next best spaces nearest to the entrance to those women who sometimes or regularly worked late. At a stroke he got the support of those of his people who felt held back by the old guard, and of the more ambitious women willing to work long hours. It also became high profile without his having to tell a soul. The old guard were in furore. They sent angry letters to human resources and senior managers in all parts of the organisation. They themselves gave him the oxygen of publicity. By the end of literally his first day his name was very high profile, he had sorted out the resisters of change from the enthusiasts and impressed on senior management his grasp of what they were looking for in terms of cultural change. Senior management congratulated themselves, modestly of course, for hiring the right person for the job.

Eleven Greatest Ideas for Getting the Basics Right

Introduction

There are many things I like about politicians, but one thing above all. They wear their ambition on their sleeves. They have absolutely no desire to hide the fact that they are playing to win, and winning means getting more and more power. They expect us to think that. They know that interviewers are certainly going to look for the politician's personal advantage in any line of thought or plan of action. They seem to relish the battle, and to pursue their careers even though they must be aware that almost all of them, from whatever height they eventually succumb, are going to be denigrated and probably despised by the lot who come next. Yet such is their vanity or their self-belief, or both, that they plunge into the war. It is easy to use words like battle and war in this context and, when you come right down to it, in the business environment as well. It is either you or someone else. One gets the glory, and the other stays in a job that firstly bores them, secondly irritates them and finally embitters them.

So, if you are in the organisation, you may as well join the *mêlée*, give ambition no ceiling and build your career. You need to stand out in the crowd and be noticed. People must see you as a cut above the rest. They must notice that you are normally right and always confident. You will make them feel their own inadequacies. This will act as a spur to those who are like you, and keeps the others in their place. How does this happen?

In the first place it is actually very easy. Get the basics right time after time after time. This chapter is about the basics. Make sure you have them in place, and then move on to deploying these techniques to your career advantage in more complex activities. Most of us think, unfortunately, that we have the basics in place and that we are doing them. 'Of course we listen, *Idea 11*, no-one is in their right mind if the customer is not at the heart of their plan *Idea 19*, and surely everyone must keep a lifetime address book *Idea 14*' we all say; but a word of caution. It is easier to describe the basics than never to fail to carry them out. Spot when your colleagues fail in them, resolve not to imitate them, and put yourself into an *élite* and quite small band of people who actually carry out their business tasks properly.

Idea 9 – Understand your starting point

Career clue

If there is something in a colleague or perhaps a customer that impresses you, work out what it is they are good at, and make it your ambition to become better than them at it.

It has been a revelation to me in preparing this book, how every successful person you speak to on the topic of career development eventually stresses the importance of preparation. Every technique you look at, from managing meetings to managing projects, starts with doing the preparatory work. About to go into a negotiation? – do your prep. Need to fire someone? – prepare for the meeting and what comes after. And so it goes on. The winner is very frequently the one who did the most effective preparation.

Take a simple example – who are you more likely to hire, someone who at the interview knows what business you are in and who your competitors are, or someone who guessed what you did and got it slightly wrong? We wouldn't think of going into an interview totally unprepared, or would we? You take risks when you play things by ear, risks that you will look foolish, that the outcome will not be to your advantage and that someone properly prepared will stand out as more competent. Even time with a customer can be wasted through bad preparation.

So, if you are not already in the habit of preparing for every phone call, meeting or other business activity, make a resolution to change. Astonishing as it may seem, this quickly puts you into the top few per cent of business people, because an awful lot of people go into meetings where their only preparation is to be absolutely determined to see what the others are going to say. Prepare properly and know your starting point.

Idea 10 – Pinpoint the destination

The next basic is to work towards objectives at all times. It is good to have a reputation for knowing what you are doing. It makes sense to know why you are doing it as well. Going to a meeting – set your objectives. Sending one of your people on a training course – set their objectives. Presenting a proposal to customers – know their objectives.

Setting clear objectives is a powerful technique for achieving success, but you need to do it well. Use the SMART acronym to check that your objectives are top quality.

- *Stretching*
  Whatever you are about to do, set a challenging objective. Everybody can achieve easy results, so stretch yourself and do better than average.
- *Measurable*
  You have not finished a good quality objective unless there is a relevant measure of success.
- *Achievable*
  Don't stretch too far. Promotion comes to people who are successful and seen to be successful. If a salesperson sells units to the value of £950,000, it is far better to do this against a target of £900,000 than the more stretching £1,000,000. The first situation is success, the second failure and both for the same actual performance. The salesperson may have gained kudos at the start of the year by being the first person to accept a million pound target, but at the end of the year no one will remember the target, just the fact that the person failed.

Career case in point

I spent some time in a selling team with a man who used not only to set objectives for a sales meeting but also think out the exact words he would like the customer to use to show that the objective had been reached. It might be the obvious 'Yes we are going to go ahead', or the softer 'Well, John, when it comes to training courses for marketing people, we will probably ask you first.' This technique gave our sales calls rifle-shot focus. It was also hilarious when the person actually did use the words. It was difficult to keep a straight face rather than jump up and punch the air with your fist.

- *Related to the customer*
  It is the contention of this book that everyone lives by selling something to a customer. Your customer may be external to the organisation for which you work, or an internal department. But they are still your customer; and your objective should always show what is in it for them as well as what is in it for you.
- *Time-targeted*
  An objective has no merit if it does not express when the measure of success should be achieved. You can subject the time target to the test of 'Is it stretching and achievable?' to finish off a thorough job.

There is one set of objectives that you should know and support, and that is your company's objectives. It is difficult to thrive and succeed in an environment that you do not like, working towards objectives you cannot identify with.

Idea 11 – Sorry, did you say something?

Active listening is a great art. The voice most people like listening to be-yond all others is their own. This is a useful aid to the ambitious who can simply do the opposite and spend a considerable part of their business life listening. If you are trying to get someone to agree to something, they will actually tell you how to do it if you ask them to talk about their require-ments and desires. In the end you are trying to link what you want to what they want – so listen, for goodness sake, and find out what it is.

I once overheard a manager talking to another just before I carried out her annual appraisal. 'I am not going to say a word', she said. 'This will be the shortest appraisal of all time.' Fat chance. I asked two open questions that enabled her to talk about that most interesting topic – her-self – and she was off. Open questions are the ones that cannot be an-swered in one word. They generally start with one of how, why, what, who, where and when. Prepare to ask a few and settle back to listen.

Listen actively. Someone described a good listener whom we both knew like this, 'He seems to give you his undivided attention.' Encourage people to talk with your body language and the occasional interjection. Listen also for what is behind what is being said. If a subordinate says 'I do not think it

Career clue

Don't leap in with your views in meetings. Listen until everyone has spoken, assimi-late what has been said and eventually summarise the substance. By that time you will know where your interests lie and be able to steer the meeting towards them.

Career clue

Suppose you are in a meeting with a colleague who is a threat or challenge to your upward mobility. Encourage him or her to direct the presentation to you by nodding and smiling in agreement. This will make them ignore the others in the room who might include your boss. If your boss is showing some disagree-ment with what is being said, the speaker might just miss the warning signal.

is necessary to take action on this', they could mean that they cannot do what is necessary or that they do not know what action to take. You will hear the difference if you polish up your listening skills, won't you. Sorry, did you say something?

Idea 12 – Deliver on time

If you think about it, you will probably agree: most business people do not do what they said they would do at the time they said they would do it. It's as simple as that. Builders are famous for finishing late, plumbers don't even start on time, and I know people who plan successfully for Virgin Trains to be twenty minutes late. Build your skills in this area. At the end of any meeting or phone call, no matter who it is with, take a note of what actions were agreed, repeat them to the other person or persons and confirm them, not just if they are important, by email. Now whatever reminder system you use, make sure it triggers off the things you agreed to do in time for you to deliver. Deliver on time and look mildly surprised if the person thanks you and expresses gratitude that you kept your word.

When something goes wrong and you cannot deliver, tell everyone as soon as you know that the delay is inevitable. Apologise and reschedule. This time put in contingency so that you do not fail again. It is much easier to deal with pressure that your delivery date is later than people would like, than it is to deal with anger when you have failed.

Career clue from the boardroom

Agree annual objectives and targets with your line manager and ensure that your delivery exceeds expectations. In other words 'Perform as Advertised.'

Sir John Collins (Chairman, National Power)

Career clue

I had a very difficult customer to whom I sold computer hardware and software solutions. We had a good product, a good enthusiastic team and our delivery was pretty good. The trouble was he used to kick a willing horse. Nothing was good enough. He complained and whinged frequently without any just cause.

I decided that he was doing it to make us maintain our performance and not get complacent, so I invented a few problems. I would call him up and say that the twenty terminals he had on order were probably going to be late; not definitely since we were going to work on it to try to get it back to the promised timescale. He would go ballistic. Talk about not listening; he shouted and bawled and went on and on. I would let him fester for a few days, and then phone him again with the news that there was no change but that we were still trying. More abuse. When finally I was ready I would phone him up and tell him I had fixed it and the first delivery date was on track.

He still complained but at least I had him diverted from where we had real problems.

Idea 13 – Deliver within budget

Hand in hand with your job is the financial expression of your success or failure. As your career progresses, the financial side will become more and more dominant. Face that as early as possible and make sure that you are developing your skills in this area as well as your technical function. We have covered the significance of delivering on time, so now you need to think about doing that without exceeding the budget. Later on we will look at how you set the right budget in the first place. Here we will give just one example of how risk and return go hand in hand, and show that if you understand the financial concept of fixed and variable costs, you are much more likely to find the best balance between the two. Risky enough to get a high return, not so risky that you have an unreasonable chance of failure.

Think of financial risk in these terms. All businesses and most departments consist of fixed and variable costs. Their fixed costs are their overheads, the people who work for them and so on. Their variable costs are those that go up or down depending on the volume of transactions or sales. A simple example is a bookshop where the fixed costs include the premises and the staff, and the variable costs the costs of the books that the customers buy. In a computer department there are fixed

---

Career case in point

An interesting paradox arises from this fixed and variable classification. When the final profit and loss account for a period is drawn up, variable costs will appear to be fixed per unit sold, while fixed costs, of course, are fixed overall but vary per unit, since they are divided among the number of units sold.

In this way it is possible to find an answer to the question, 'How can we improve our profits without selling more units or reducing our fixed or variable costs?' The answer is to make more units even though you do not sell them.

What happens is that you build up inventory. The value of each unit that goes into inventory is its variable cost plus its share of the fixed costs. You do not account for the expenses of the unit until you sell it. So profits have gone up because the fixed costs have been divided into more units.

So, the next time you see a car manufacturer whose chairman's statement includes the words, 'We increased our profits this year despite a difficult year for sales of new vehicles', check how many new vehicles are parked on the factory forecourt.

costs in providing the service to users, and variable costs according to the usage that the customers make.

This concept is central to the measurement of profits, and therefore to the measurement of 'within budget'. The movement of costs from fixed into variable tends to reduce risks and also reduce return. If, for example, you pay a salesperson salary and commission, then salary is in fixed costs and commission is variable. If you offer to pay a higher rate of commission but a lower salary, you have reduced your fixed costs. If the salesperson does well and over-performs target, then you will get less profit, but you have reduced your fixed costs and therefore your risk. If you do not understand this, you can get blind-sided by the finance department into thinking you are operating less profitably or with more risk than you planned.

There are three key issues to delivering within budget:

- Get your initial budget right. If this gives you problems because it will give such a high estimate of costs or low estimate of profit that there is doubt about the continuation of your department or the existence of your project, then plan for the cost overrun to come about a quarter after you have moved on.
- Make sure your monitoring system gives ample warning of budget problems to come. Use a red, amber, green status report to ensure this.
- Understand your management accounting system so that firstly, it is a correct reflection of the value you are adding, and secondly, that you can use it to maximise the perceived added value.

Idea 14 – Keep a lifetime address book

Some companies give such a value to their database of knowledge on customers and prospective customers that they quantify it and put it on the balance sheet as an intangible asset. I quite understand this, although some would argue with their accountants. Companies have changed hands because one bought another for its mar-

Career case in point

A man who was on a training course that my colleague John ran some fifteen years ago rang him up recently. Since the man was in the delegate section of his address book, John was able to demonstrate a remarkable memory. He also had the opinions of himself and the other managers running the course on how good they thought the man was at the time. All of this is invaluable as he has now become a senior manager and is now one of John's prospective clients.

ket information, and mergers have taken place where the only real synergy is having complementary customer lists. The individual manager's version of this is his or her address book. Never take anyone off it. You never know when they might come in useful. Organise it in sections so that you have a reminder of where and with what purpose you met the person.

I have never met anyone who has kept a long-term address book say that it has been a waste of time. I have heard many regret that they didn't. I'm one of them dammit.

Idea 15 – 'There's an expensive rebel – time'

The next line of this quotation from Thomas Flatman runs: 'And in his squadrons Poverty.' Careerists are busy by definition. You may be brilliant at delegating, but you still need to be busy – as well as *look* busy – if you are to elbow your way forward. You must make the best use of your time.

Earlier we said that you need to set realistic objectives and aims if you are to stand a good chance of achieving them. The next step towards realism in using your time is to prioritise, first your objectives, and then the actions within those objeclives. Prioritising in itself takes time but is the start of the cure for the poor time manager. If you have problems in this area, then 'prioritise' is a piece of advice you have probably heard many times. It is also advice that may not cut much ice with the person who has started to miss out the slice of toast in the morning in order to get to the office earlier. Everything seems urgent. However, prioritising objectives and then regularly monitoring those priorities is a valuable method of learning to use your time effectively. It will help you to focus on a few clear areas and steer the way to effective time management.

The simple genius behind prioritising is to decide what is important to you, and behave accordingly. You can become your own consultant; realistically setting targets, keeping accountable to yourself and ensuring an efficient use of time. If you need a technique for this, there is no shortage. Some people recommend the ABC approach, where you attach A for urgent activities, B for less urgent and C for the rest. My own experience of this is that I only mark activities with a C if there is little likelihood of my doing them at all. Perhaps a numbering system of 1–10 might work better.

Career clue from the boardroom

Always do unpleasant jobs at the earliest opportunity, but do plan carefully how to execute them. There is nothing more distracting than having an unpleasant job hanging over you. They seldom turn out to be as nasty as you anticipate and there is always a sense of relief having completed an unpleasant job.

George Paul (Chairman, Norwich Union)

I mentioned this comment to a friend of mine who, while agreeing with its message, said that right now he had to prioritise his unpleasant jobs. 'To get round to a pleasant one would indeed be a relief', he mourned.

In the long term what you are trying to do is to move forward your attention to issues to a time before they become a crisis. The measures of urgency and impact are useful here. If a problem has high urgency and if unattended will have a high impact on your performance, it plainly requires attention now. The well-organised manager tries to pay attention next to issues that have a high impact but are not yet urgent. Planning what to do about a problem before it becomes urgent is a major stress cutter and time-management aid.

Technology ought to help. Email may be a great time saving device but it has to be handled correctly. We must not become slaves to our email; if it is the first thing that you check in the morning and takes well over an hour to read and reply to, slavery threatens. One of the simple principles to remember in using email is that you get as much as you send. Think carefully about the amount of unnecessary e-mail you yourself send. Ask yourself; does this really need to be said now? Is this the most effective means of communication for the current situation? As a guideline, send as few as possible to do the job and still have a life. Try it for a week. Send out as few as you dare, copying almost nobody and then enjoy the diminution of your in-box.

'Nearly 110 million people now use email, collectively receiving 7 trillion messages annually', according to the Electronic Messaging Association. What on earth do they all say? Advice from those in the know is that email should not be used to communicate the complex, new ideas, issues requiring clarification, solicitation for agreement, the emotionally charged or material that has a strong personal impact on the recipient.

Email is, after all, just another office tool. Checking your email more than two or three times per day is, in the words of a recent law graduate, 'sad'. But, of course, she had to add, 'Unless you are expecting a very important message.' Mmm.

Do not fool yourself into thinking that the world is split into filers and non-filers and that it is the non-filers who are destined for greater things. When you're in control of the desk, office, files and resources you've assembled, you are more likely to achieve focus and effectiveness. Much time is lost looking for and rewriting or recollecting materials. Plan your filing system for the long term. Be as methodical as possible, pedantic if you can face it. A friend of my daughter who spent one university vacation doing filing is determined to become king and abolish the use of the alphabet in filing systems. According to him we should use colour and musical associations to locate groups of materials. But until he has done that, a numbered and alphabetically organised system is a must for the person looking to make use of that unrecyclable resource – time, with its attendant threat of poverty.

Idea 16 – Learn to count, make the most of annual reports

Many people underestimate the amount of useful information held in an annual report. Many people overestimate it as well; it is of course three months out of date when it is published, and it has been doctored and spun until the exact words are found that paint the picture, good or bad, that management wants the world to look at. But they are still a rich source of ammunition for the career-minded. If you learn to be able to read them in a short period of preparation time, you will set yourself up for a lot of the financial and managerial tasks that lie ahead.

The skill of speed reading an annual report is useful in a number of ways:

- If you are applying for a job in an industry related to yours but not exactly the same one, it can be a crash course to prepare for the interview.
- If you are about to do business with a new industry sector, whether you are buying from it or selling to it, annual reports give you the key issues and measures of companies in the industry.
- At all times reading the annual report of your competitors is part of the vital task of knowing the enemy, (and potential employer).
- If you look after your own pension, or want to build a portfolio of shares by regular saving, it is a source of data.

So how do you do it quickly? Start not with the figures but with the reports from the chairman and directors. From these you should be able to devise a simple matrix showing what their trading strategy is. What products and services do they sell to what markets. (There is more of this in *if you want to get ahead, get a strategy Idea 40.*) Now look at their history, and strategy if they talk about it, for mergers and acquisitions. This will tell you something of the shape of their business, and incidentally whether the bit you are interested in is safely located in their long-term strategy rather than their little group of embarrassing difficulties in the out tray. Finally you should now know what they regard as their competitive edge.

Move then from the strategy to the numbers. One of the directors will have expressed an opinion on their past year's performance on sales and profit. Do the ratios back this up? Remember it is almost always the delta that tells you of a company's health. This year's figures are not much good without last year's for comparison purposes. Indeed most reports give you a five or ten year history of the numbers, a very useful chart of their past. It may include some financial ratios, but how these are calculated can vary from one company to another; so in the long term you should learn how to calculate them for yourself.

Why do you need these ratios? The strategy has told you of the long-term intentions of the company. The financial ratios tell you firstly if the strategy has been successful in the past, and secondly whether or not the current strategy can be supported by the financial situation the company is in. You need profits to invest in new markets, for example, and you also need cash. Do not confuse the two. If you are going to expand by buying companies, you need quick access to cash, possibly in large amounts. You need quick access to cash because takeovers are generally built on a sudden opportunity. A competitor makes a serious mistake, produces a profit warning to their shareholders and their share price plunges. At that point a takeover becomes a possibility, and a company that has immediate access to cash is in a better position to act fast than one that has not. As a final example, if the board has said that its spend on research and development is an important ingredient of its strategy, then you need to be able to see what it spent last year, the proportion that that was of its profits, and whether it is becoming more or less easy to maintain the spend into the future.

The financial ratios that give you the answers to the questions raised by the strategy of all companies include looking at profitability. Here are three measures of this that have a widespread usefulness across a lot of industries.

- *Sales and profit growth*
  By what percentage did sales grow last year, and did profits at least keep pace with this growth? You will almost always find these numbers in the financial highlights section at the very beginning of the report. It is quite possible for a business to show low growth from time to time but not in the long term. It is also possible to have much higher sales growth one year than profit growth, but only for a short time. It is much more comfortable to work in a business where profits are going up faster than sales.
- *Return on capital employed*
  The ratio of net profit before tax to the long-term capital, share capital and loan capital, used by the business. You may find this in the report or you may have to calculate it. Compare it with last year and check that your interpretation of the health of the business is the same as the directors'. Are the profits there to support any plans for expansion? Some industries produce return on capital employed of above twenty per cent, in others fifteen per cent may be a good performance. We will see in a moment how to find out which is appropriate.
- *Profit margin*
  This is the ratio of net profit before tax to sales. If this has gone down, you need to find out why. The problem could be in one of two main places. Either the cost of producing the products and services that the company sold has gone up, reducing the gross profit margin; or the company's expenses in ad-

ministration and selling have risen faster than sales growth. The former is often caused by competitive pressure on prices, the latter by expansion of the fixed costs of the business.

There are other profitability ratios, and some of these may be more relevant to the industry you are studying. You will eventually find out what they are, particularly if you use the annual reports of competitors. There will be common measures that they all emphasise.

Next we want to know about the availability and cost of the capital in the business. There are some interesting implications if a company relies principally on debt to finance itself. If interest rates go up, then that will damage a big borrower's profits. Debt has to be repaid, and if there is a lull in profits one year, that could give a highly geared company, one with a lot of debt compared with shareholders' equity, a problem with cash. To understand the capital position look at the gearing ratios. There are two that give you what you want.

Using the very simple ratio of long-term debt as a percentage of shareholders' funds plus long-term debt, low gearing is less than 10%, medium gearing is about 33% and high gearing is about 66%. If a company has low gearing at the moment, it is in a position to borrow, for example for acquisition purposes, without becoming too highly geared. It has good access to cash.

Another popular measure of gearing is *income gearing*. If you calculate the ratio of interest payable as a percentage of earnings before interest and tax, then low gearing is less than 25%, medium gearing is between 26% and 75%, and high gearing is above 75%.

For small and medium sized companies you might have to look at liquidity. This is simply the ability of a company to pay its bills. Again two ratios will tell you what you need to know about this.

The *current ratio* is the ratio of current assets to current liabilities. By definition, current assets will be turned into cash within a year, and current liabilities are bills that must be paid in the same timescale, so a comparison of the two shows the

Career case in point

You will hear people talking of financial leverage. This shows how managers can use debt to make 'leveraged' profits. It is a neat idea, but has the downside that if debt exaggerates an increase in profits, it does the same to a decrease. Suppose a company has earnings before interest and tax of 100 and has an interest bill of 60 then the profits attributable to shareholders would be 40. Here is the effect of financial leverage on the same company.

	10% Increase	10% decrease
Earnings before interest and tax	110	90
Interest payable	60	60
Profit for shareholders	50	30

In both cases the 10% change in earnings has had a 25% impact on the profit available for shareholders.

liquidity of the business. It is comfortable to have £1.50 in current assets for every £1 in debt, more difficult if the ratio is 1.0, and the company could be in a mess if the ratio drops below that.

For the *quick ratio*, you take the current ratio and deduct stock, also called *inventory* from the current assets. This is to allow for the fact that stock will not definitely be sold and turned into cash. It depends on the nature of the business, of course, with fashion goods the most unreliable in this respect. You can see the cash difficulties of the company when the quick ratio drops far below 1.0.

These financial measures are useful to most organisations. Also useful are measures of the utilisation of assets. What return does the company earn from its assets?

How good is the company at getting its customers to pay their bills? How quickly does stock leave the warehouse after it arrived? And so on. But these are more specific to particular industries, and you will have to find out which measures of asset utilisation are important for the company you are studying if you want to go into more depth. For more information on all of this, read *Smart Things to Know about Business Finance* by Ken Langdon and Alan Bonham (Capstone, 2000).

You have now learnt from an annual report what the strategy of a company is, and whether the financial measures support that strategy or make it unlikely to succeed. You also know whether the situation is getting better or worse, because you have compared last year's with this year's figures. But you do not know how this company compares with others in the same industry sector. To do this, you can of course get hold of their annual reports and do the same thing. Indeed if you are talking about your own industry, this is a very good idea. It pays to know the competition. You can also refer to books on industry averages. Available in any business library, such books have taken each industry sector, analysed the ratios for each company in the sector and produced an industry average. It is straightforward to compare the company you are studying with that average.

With a bit of practice you will be able to use annual reports as a source of business intelligence and as first-class preparatory work when you are starting to deal with a new company.

Idea 17 – Don't fence yourself in

All business is a combination of strategic planning, operational efficiency and opportunism. Just as when you have a specific plan for what products you sell to what markets, you will nevertheless accept a query from a different market if it is a good enough opportunity; so it is with your career. You want to be, as far as you can, available for another role. If an opportunity means a change to the competition, this should not pose a problem. But in your own organisation beware of unnecessary barriers to upward mobility. The principal difficulty you face is projects. It is a good idea to take on projects, either one-off events or projects to do with changing how the company goes about its business. But it is a sensible rule of most project sponsors that the project manager should commit himself or herself to the project for its duration. I suppose this pushes you towards taking on shorter projects. Run the annual production team conference rather than take responsibility for building the new head office. So when you are defining your strategy, see *if you want to get ahead, get a strategy Idea 40*; and improving your operational efficiency, don't forget to be continuously on the lookout for opportunities.

This is not to say that you should not set yourself broad goals. You will find that an overview goal will impact how you behave now. Your plan should be like the outside edge of a jigsaw, it keeps you within your boundaries but allows you to fill the picture in whatever order you want. For example, suppose you want, during your career, to spend some time in a hot country. Don't tie yourself down to one place. You will, then, when the opportunity arises, take a decision that gets you to the hot country but is also appropriate for your career. The fact that you have an overall goal makes you ask questions and talk to people differently. That way you learn from other people's experience the best way to go.

Career clue from the boardroom

Think carefully how you can make your boss's life easier. There is always a risk that your boss may come to rely upon you so much that he or she is reluctant to recommend you for promotion; but that is a risk worth taking in the quest to raise your profile in your boss's estimate.

George Paul (Chairman, Norwich Union)

Idea 18 – Know the competition

There are two arguments about pursuing a career in an organisation. Either stick with the devil you know and plough your furrow through the one you start with, or be flexible and willing to move to a competitor. The main logic of the first approach is that once you have got the hang of making one organisation work for you, why go to the trouble and risk of finding out how another one operates. And it is true that you do find the short cuts and the people who can help through experience. When something goes wrong it is easier to put it right if you know who can do it and that they owe you a favour.

I have certainly seen people from a strong culture find it very hard to adapt to the totally different culture that allows much more individualism. Many people from IBM, for example, found it hard to believe that so much was left to them in the other outfits they joined. Where they expected to find a system or a lever they could pull to make something happen they found nothing, and some of them did not thrive as a result.

But a career is not only about performance it is about power and influence and money. So I come down heavily on the side of flexibility of employers. After all, you may very well be able to miss out a rung of the ladder if you join a competitor by leapfrogging one level as you join. So plan to tack your way to the top. Your career is in your industry not in your organisation.

As well as knowing the company by studying published material, work out how to become known by the competition. Perhaps there are some trade organisations where you will meet them in a forum with a common purpose. Volunteer for this, and look good in front of them. Network with them at trade conventions, or if you happen to meet them at a customer's premises or on a training course. You never know when such activity might bear fruit.

Idea 19 – The customer is king – alleluia!

'Through here pass the most important people in the world – our customers.' This notice is above the door of one of the worst garage workshops through which it has been my dubious pleasure to pass. The thought is right. Everyone has customers on whom they depend for their livelihood. You will put yourself into the top echelons of business managers if you actually deliver on that statement and treat the customer as king. There is no cynical get-out on this. You can take all the short cuts in the world, but in the end your career depends on your customers doing business with you and expressing their delight with your performance. Make them drive every stage of your plan. Try to think ahead of what they will require in the future. There are two kinds of manager in this respect; those who are always trying to catch up because they become aware of changes in their customer's needs after the event, and those who make changes in anticipation of this. When you are thus ahead of the game, it will be difficult for anything to stop your success. I'd love to creep up in the dead of night and change that sign to 'Through here pass the most incompetent people in the world – your managers.'

Career clue from the Boardroom

These days up-and-coming managers should take every opportunity for advanced education and training and also recognise the need for 'soft' skills such as sociability at work. Most importantly they must become increasingly accomplished in customer science, because business deregulation and the subsequent emergence of a highly competitive global market, means that companies must be truly driven by the needs and preferences of the customer. The manager who understands this and puts effective, appropriate strategies into play will succeed.

Lord Marshall of Knightsbridge (Chairman, Invensys)

Seven Greatest Ideas for Getting a New Job

Introduction

During your career you are bound to change jobs, whether you are struggling up your own organisation or jumping ship to another. Indeed it is a bad idea to stay in one place for too long. For a start, if you stay around for a while, something is bound to go badly wrong. And you are going to get new jobs fast if you take this book's advice and concentrate on execution; that is getting things done. You can buy in ideas and strategies if the worst comes to the worst, but it is execution that gets noticed. A series of completed targets and projects is the best path to the next leap forward. But it is also necessary to keep on your toes. Make sure your CV is readable *Idea 20*, truthful *Idea 22*, and up to date so that you can simply edit it into the

---

Career clue

In some businesses you may have to think quite a long time ahead to get to the job you want. A pilot came out of the RAF and wanted to fly for BA. He went to the trouble, in his preparatory work, to get to know every relevant airline and the details of their fleets. From their order book, he knew that BA would need 40 pilots for a certain aircraft. He also knew that they tended to poach their pilots from British Midland (BM). He applied to BM to get this aircraft rating and was successful. Some time later the BA headhunters came to call and he got the job he wanted.

appropriate state when an opportunity comes along. It goes without saying that you must be good at the gateway to most jobs: the interview *Idea 24*.

Idea 20 – Write a readable CV

I think the case is won now for starting your CV with your current position and going backwards until you get to primary school. Check for relevance. 'Is this item going to help them to know that I am well suited to the job?' When you apply for your first job you probably do need to include things you have been president of at school or college, but drop that lot out later on; unless, of course, you are deliberately climbing up the old school tie.

Nowadays it is very easy for the presentation of the document to be first class, so anything else is a suicide note. Well-spaced, short and to the point is what you need. Make sure it is also in pristine condition every time. I was looking through a pile of CVs for a client recently and found one that looked shabbier and more frequently presented than an old actor's cheque. It was difficult for us to take the candidate seriously. That is the point of CVs. They are your silent salesperson when you are not there.

How complete to make your CV is up to you, but you do not have to put anything on it that may damage your case. You can probably miss out the wrong job that lasted only six months, and a slight exaggeration of your role in your present company may help your chances of getting a more senior job with a competitor. But beware: *don't lie on your CV Idea 22*.

If you believe that your application form will have to stand out in a shoal of others, you may need to resort to gimmick. These go from the simple, use a bigger size of paper like American quarto, to the complex. Where, for example, you are applying for a creative job in the media, you could send it in on a video, or carve your name in a potato stencil.

Career case in point

A young relative of mine was applying for her first job out of university. Although she was not certain that a career in journalism was right for her, she had decided to apply for a graduate trainee job in a newspaper publisher just in case. To the question 'What newspapers and periodicals do you regularly read?', she had replied confidently, and I am sure honestly, 'None.' Now, I am no expert in human resources, but even I knew that that was not the ideal response.

Idea 21 – Keep the application form relevant

For most jobs you will have to fill in an application form. Most of this will be standard, but watch out for the less formal questions that will give a signal one way or the other for your suitability to this particular job. Keep the readers in mind and what they are looking for.

Idea 22 – Don't lie on your CV

It is very flattering to get headhunted. Suppose that one telephones you and arranges to meet you outside office hours. They discuss the job with you and you decide it is pretty much just what you are looking for. When it comes to filling in the application form or presenting the headhunter with your CV, you realise that an assumption the headhunter has made is not true. You spoke about your time at Birmingham University without actually mentioning that you got a pass degree. And yet everything else seems so right for both you and the employer. Are you tempted to claim a 2:1? Well, if it was risky before, it is even more risky now particularly for people who graduated after 1995. That is the base year that the credit reference company Experian will use in compiling a complete list of degree results. The company did a deal with the UK's universities and will make this information available, for a fee, to employers who are becoming increasingly aware that little lies on a CV can prove crucial to the applicant's ability to do the job.

It may only be a little lie but look where it could lead. Jeffrey Archer went from changing the name of the school he attended to persuading a friend to lie to a court, and then he couldn't apply for the job he wanted.

In any case the chances of getting caught out in mistakes of fact is probably high enough for you to decide to deal with the truth and nothing but the truth. Nobody said you had to tell the whole truth. People who are not consistent liars, but try it out during a job interview, are frequently unable to stop their body language clearly telling an experienced HR person that they are feeling uncomfortable. And once a lie is discovered, you have blown the interview and your chances of working for this employer.

According to the *Guardian*, there is certainly a market for the Experian service, since research has shown that a quarter of all CVs contain lies. And yet most firms do not test for skills. So it is quite possible to get away with an exaggeration of your computer or other skills but still very dangerous if you need these skills from day one. The humiliation when your boss and colleagues reveal your deception will make it a very rough start. And you cannot be sure who is going to read your CV. Employers are increasingly turning to recruitment consultants as the first filter, and these people are much more likely to test for skills.

So if the job seems ideal for you, and you seem ideal for the job, don't pretend to meet a criterion set by the employer, rather work out in your preparatory work why the criterion is unnecessary and how quickly you could become able to fulfil it in any case. A lie never ceases to be a ticking time bomb. The discovery of the pass degree even after a lot of time in the new job is still damaging. And it's so easy to forget what you said if it wasn't the truth.

Idea 23 – Get on-line

There are many ways of using the Internet to help with getting a new job. Here are two:

- Scroll through the employment pages and then use the web page of the company you are interested in to get yourself ready. You can further improve your preparatory work if you also look at the sites of the company's competitors. (The Internet is also useful in this respect for finding out about what your competitors are doing when you have got the job. It is nice and anonymous, and you can get information sent to your home.) Look for job sites and use on-line communities for networking.
- Send your CV and application form by e-mail to show that you are up to date with the technology. Send a hard copy version as well, because e-mail often screws up formatting and you want them to be looking at a well-presented document as the team prepares for your interview.

Career clue from the Boardroom

People possess different aspirations, capability and motivation to inform their decisions about career development. In recognition of this, the best advice to help individuals build a future that meets their needs is to 'know yourself'. In NatWest, we provide a considerable amount of support to our staff through the use of appraisal and development systems, psychometric testing, development centres and other technologies to help them develop this understanding. Equipped with this knowledge, they are better placed to make decisions about what is right for them.

Chris Wathen (Director of Human Resources, NatWest Group)

Chris Wathen could have added that the bank is also better placed to make decisions about the member of staff. So, be prepared; pre-empt any employer's use of profiling. Available on the Internet now are self-profiling packages. They are easy to find and cheap to buy. You go on-line, fill in the form and get in return the sort of assessment that employers would get. Knowing the sort of result you are likely to get may change the data you give the program, since you will want to accentuate the positive and so on. After all, practice makes perfect.

Idea 24 – Don't ring us, we'll ring you: interview well

The interview is used very extensively to sieve out internal and external candidates for jobs. So you need to be good at them. You can view all meetings as rehearsals for interviews, but there are some techniques peculiar to interviews to which you should give some thought. First of all, remember that people make up their minds about most candidates in the first few minutes, or if it is negative, seconds. So look right for the job you are going for, and look as though you have taken some trouble in your personal and business preparation. Don't be late for an interview or look hot and sweaty from having to rush to get there.

Think through and role-play with a friend or colleague the answers to the obvious questions. Have an interesting short *précis* of your strengths and weaknesses. Back the strengths up with examples of where they have stood you in good stead. Make sure that the weaknesses do not invalidate your application for this particular job.

Be able to describe yourself. Fix on the type of person that the job description and any other material you have been given requires, and give good reasons for meeting the spec plus a bit more. Do it sensitively, of course; a lot of people do not like arrogance, and no one likes complacency. Don't, in this regard, score points off the interviewers particularly if you have better qualifications than they do. You do not have to ram it down their throat that you went to Oxford; they are already impressed. Keep your name-dropping subtle.

Know as much about the people who will be there as you can; and this goes for the company and its competitors too. The answer to 'Why do you want to work for this company?' is much more impressive if you are able to support what you say with reference to a competitor's disadvantage. Anecdotes are only useful if they are relevant.

We will look at the interview again in *appraise yourself well Idea 33*.

Idea 25 – Have good references and referees

I am told by usually reliable sources that more and more recruitment agencies and employers are actually going to the trouble of taking up references. Make sure then that someone who has allowed you to use their name knows enough that is relevant to the job in question to be useful when called. That is again the clue. It is not necessarily useful to have someone saying how good you are with the local scout troop, if they cannot, or will not, relate that to the world of work.

Relevance comes from the industry and from knowing you in the business world. A referee in one of the company's clients would not go down badly.

Idea 26 – Remember the big picture re salary

Particularly at the start of your career, keep in mind that the rewards of getting to the top are very substantial, and that if it means accepting small potatoes to begin with, the game is still worth the candle. Don't whinge about your early salary; rather tell yourself that you are investing for the

Career clue from the boardroom

You might be better off doing an extra few months at £20,000 a year, rather than causing grief by bellyaching. The eventual return could be well worth it.

Adman earning £1 million a year

future. Agree to small or no rises and even no promotions for the first couple of years then go for the big hike when you have something to argue with.

I was working in a theatre once when an assistant stage manager did a bunk with the £100 she had been given to buy props. 'What a mug,' said a more seasoned ASM, 'If she had waited a bit longer she could have gone off with five times that.' So it is in business. Only the people with little or no vision fiddle their expenses for a couple of pints in the pub, or charge for a first-class train fare and sit in standard class. This is short sighted in many ways. I mean who do you need to impress who sits in standard class?

*E*ight *G*reatest *I*deas for *S*tanding *O*ut in the *C*rowd

Introduction

We have already agreed that the competition is sitting next to you. Only so many can climb the greasy pole, and as soon as possible you want to start looking like a likely high-flier. Attracting favourable attention is something you have to keep up at every level until you reach the top. Perhaps you will want to stand out even in that rather sparse crowd, and there is some advice on that in the last two sections. But for the moment getting noticed is what it is all about. Some of it is simple: *know your boss's diary Idea 29*, is a good case in point. Sometimes it is tricky, like choosing friends *Idea 31*, and avoiding association with failure *Idea 30*; but let's start with one of the ways that, by definition, you can stand out from the crowd.

Idea 27 – Present yourself well

If you have a natural talent for making presentations and you can enjoy them once the nervousness has worn off, you put yourself ahead of the crowd. In some company cultures, indeed, you are pretty much on a slow track if your skills at presentations are poor or if you look scared witless at the end of the presentation as well as at the beginning. At an early stage in your career, volunteer to be the person who presents the results of a workshop, or makes a presentation on some new topic to the departmental meeting.

   If you are not a natural at this game, go on training until you can at least survive, although I do know one senior manager who made it to the top and remained

---

Example

I had no idea of how useful presentations were until this incident happened to me. In the dark ages of the seventies, the business world was burdened with a new tax – Value Added Tax. I was a graduate trainee at the time and my boss, who sometimes found it difficult to think of constructive things for a rookie to do, asked if I could have a look at this VAT business and make a presentation of what it was about to the next area meeting. I got hold of government papers and found the concept of the tax hard to understand.

I persevered and spoke to a load of people, including government people, who were helpful. At last I was able to understand how the tax worked in my terms. These were, of course, the terms that my colleagues in the area would also use. By luck I heard a joke on the radio about VAT inspectors being called 'Vatman and Robin', so I nicked that and used it as a running gag through the presentation. It went well and I knew that it had done my career no harm at all.

My boss mentioned that it had gone well to his boss, who told him that he had attended a presentation by some accountants on the tax and that no one in the audience had understood a word of it. I was asked to give the same presentation at my boss's boss's team meeting. Very useful, high profile stuff.

---

a complete liability on his feet. When asked how he did it he replied, 'Ducking and weaving, old boy, I avoided the things like the plague.'

Funnily enough the usual suspects are the best tips for making effective presentations. Set tight objectives and talk exclusively in the terms of the audience. Try not to talk to mixed audiences. It can be difficult to make the same presentation both to the marketing people and to research and development at the same time, even though the topic is of mutual interest.

> **Career clue from the boardroom**
>
> Presentations are about *them*, the audience, rather than *you* the speaker. It actually makes you look better when you are talking about them.
>
> Richard Humphreys (serial Chairman)

It is a very good idea to announce the objectives at the start of the presentation. The audience then knows where you are going to take them. Some people avoid this since you do run the risk that someone in the audience will say that it will not be possible for you to achieve your objectives. Logically it is better to know this at the start of the presentation than at the end. Who knows, if you know what the audience's objections are, you may be able to use the presentation itself to overcome them.

Think about your preparation in three areas:

- the structure of the content or argument;
- the mechanics of the room and the visual aids; and
- your personal delivery.

Structure

Before you start, make sure that it is the right time to make the presentation in the first place. Quite often you could achieve your objectives in some other way that costs less and possibly has less risk. Mind you, if the point of the presentation is to raise your profile, then ignore this advice. Make sure also that you have done everything possible before the presentation that can help to achieve the objectives. Getting the most senior person on your side before you begin is a good idea. Finally make sure you know your audience well enough. What will motivate them to think your idea a good one? What is in it for them? Aim at making effective presentations as well as elegant ones, and use your performance on the day to give it a theatrical edge.

Now prepare the background to the presentation. Who asked you to do this? Who have you talked to, and who has helped you? Cover also whose agreement you already have to what you are proposing. The audience should now be aware of how well qualified you are to talk to them on this topic.

Now state the problem or opportunity that you are addressing. You are there to agree that you and your audience have a problem and you have the solution, or that they have an opportunity and you know how to exploit it. If it is difficult to express your purpose as a problem or opportunity, then you have not set your objective specifically enough.

Now comes the clever bit of preparation that will set your work ahead of the crowd. Get the audience to understand, and if possible agree the 'basis of decision' that they should use in looking at your solution. This is a much more subtle way of selling an idea than banging on about the features of your solution. The basis of decision you suggest will, of course, describe your solution. You are then able at a later time to say simply 'And my suggested action plan meets the basis of decision we spoke about (or agreed) at the beginning of this session.' The more interactive you keep this part, and the more it appears that they have built their own basis of decision, the more likely you are to get their agreement.

Now reveal your solution. Do it in their terms, illustrate it with examples and make sure that at the end of this section the audience will be able to describe exactly how things will be if they adopt your idea.

Now hit them with the benefits. These are the business and personal benefits they will get from your proposal. Now they should know what is in it for them.

Career clue

Always ride your luck, in presentations and in all aspects of your career. If a point has gone down well, consider if you need to work on that one and drop some other points that you have prepared.

If you are presenting to a customer or prospect, don't mistime the delivery of the section on why they should do business with your particular company. No one is in the least bit interested in your company unless they have provisionally decided that they want to adopt your solution. I am therefore convinced that you should never do the 'why my company' fanfare until someone in the audience has asked, 'Why should we go with you on this one?' or words to that effect. Similarly it is good technique to say to the enquirer, 'What would you like to know about our organisation?' even if you have a well-prepared pitch. This helps you to tailor your pitch to what the audience thinks is important rather than what you think is important. Sorry to bang on, but I have seen more presentations ruined by overselling the presenter's company at the wrong time than by any other misdemeanour.

The time has come to close for agreement. Make sure you can spell out the next one or two steps that need to be carried out to make progress. If they agree to your future plan, they have agreed with your suggestion.

Career clue

Be open to new ideas. Even if you have spent a lot of time preparing a presentation, you should still listen to your audience and be ready to accept an alternative idea if it is better than yours.

Mechanics

More can go wrong with the mechanics of a presentation than you would believe. I have seen people arrive with visual aids that the room did not have the facilities to show. I have seen piles of overhead projector slides dropped and mixed up, flipchart stands falling over, overhead projector slides slowly curling up until they display nothing and so on. The main messages here are: keep it simple, know the room, and rehearse in it beforehand if possible.

Next get the timing right. People do not like presentations going on beyond the time allowed, particularly if you are one item on an agenda. Plan your timing to get to the future plan well before the end of the time allocated. Three quarters of the way through is perfect, since you then have time to deal with questions and objections. No audience likes to be told to keep their questions to the end. Why should they? If they need an answer to follow your drift they need to ask the question.

If there is more than one speaker at the same meeting there are some further hazards, which is why I much prefer to work on my own. Make sure every speaker has compared notes, and that they are all there for the whole presentation. An audience loves nothing more than one speaker contradicting something a previous speaker said.

Be prepared for the questions you will be asked and objections that will be raised. It is excellent technique to role-play the audience's questions with a colleague at rehearsal time. You will find that you have practised eighty per cent of the questions if you do, and will produce much smoother and more convincing answers as a result. If someone asks a silly question, the rest of the audience will be aware of this and laugh, outwardly or inwardly, at his or her foolishness. Don't add to their discomfort by scoring a witty point off their stupidity. Funnily enough, this brings the audience back on to the questioner's side and makes them regard you as the sort of person who kicks a person when they are down.

Finally, rehearsal is not optional. If you rush in to give the usual pitch to a new audience without thinking it through and rehearsing, it will look exactly as though that is what you have done.

Presentations have great potential to give good return to the careerist, but as usual they carry the consequent risk. Most of this risk is in the mechanics of the event.

Career clue

If I have to pick just two pieces of advice for business presentations, I would say 'Rehearsal with the role-playing of the question and answer session, and the use of visual aids that are pictures rather than words or figures'.

Anthony Jay (Creator of *Yes, Minister*)

Delivery

Strange as it may seem, if you set good objectives and get the structure and mechanics right, your delivery will not be the make or break of the presentation. This is why many people who do not regard themselves as natural performers can give effective presentations time after time. If you are using the right words in the right order and your visual aids work, most of the battle is done. But there are some rules of thumb that can be useful.

The first of these is to check that the talk is interesting – really interesting – to the audience not just to you. This rule tends to make presentations shorter rather than longer. The old comic's maxim 'always leave them wanting more' holds good in business life. Do not go on if you have achieved your objective. Just because you have prepared another five slides, you do not have to use them. I have seen people unsell an idea by going on after they had received agreement to their proposition.

Use spoken rather than written English and try to vary your voice. If you have a tendency to be monotonous, use more than one type of visual aid to gain variety. Move around; sit down from time to time; do anything to keep the audience's attention.

Making the audience laugh is a good thing; telling jokes in the manner of 'I wonder if you have heard the one about …' is bad. Always weave yourself into the story. You met the person who said … or you were in the train with a man who …

Career clue from the boardroom

Polish your presentation skills. Everything can be learned, and we live in a superficial world. So make sure you are superficially good. You are more likely to make impact with style rather than substance.

Richard Humphreys (serial Chairman)

Even if it is an outrageous gag that you could not possibly have witnessed, they will enjoy the story much more than if you raise a huge sign post saying 'Joke coming'.

Finally check your delivery for the abstract and avoid it. Talk in simple concrete terms and don't pad it out in any way. Avoid the slow track of poor presenters by following these simple rules of persuasive communication.

Idea 28 – Wear eye-catching and/or unusual clothes

This advice is not for the faint-hearted. You should avoid looking like everyone else. How eccentric you choose to be depends to some extent on the culture of the organisation you work for. If the first thing the partners know about you is that you wear bow ties, you have made your point. Some of them, however, may not like it, but this could very well be compensated by the fact that you have been noticed. I once trained a man in a leading telecommunications company who wore eccentric clothes with corduroy a main ingredient along with expansive and brightly coloured braces. In the nature of the training course I had to ask the question, 'What do you think your clothes say about you?' He responded, 'They say that although I have got

---

Career clue from the Boardroom

I suppose the single overall message I would give is 'have the courage to stand out in the crowd.' In many large companies it is all too easy for young managers trying to find their corporate feet to adopt a low profile. They might be effective, but their individual efforts could also be invisible. If aspiring managers wish to be selected for advancement, they have to signal their intent and be seen.

Lord Marshall of Knightsbridge (Chairman, Invensys)

to a senior job in your organisation, you will never own me.' I could not argue with that.

Idea 29 – Know your boss's diary

There is a piece of advice that has been going the rounds for years – make sure you know what you would say to the chairman, of your company or your customer's, if you met them by chance in the lift. Most of us are like rabbits caught in the headlights and waste the one to two minute window of time with small talk. There is a clue here for the careerist. But it is broader than just the chairman.

Career clue from the boardroom

If you know your boss's diary, you will know when they are talking to people to whom you would like exposure. First prepare. If you did get the opportunity what would you say? The objective, almost certainly, is simply to be invited to meet with the person for any reason under the sun. So, you know what you would say; now engineer the opportunity to say it. The best way is simply to breeze in. 'Oh, I'm sorry I didn't realise ...' 'That's all right,' says your boss, 'come in and meet Lord so-and-so.' He or she will probably add more in terms of a quick description of what you do for the organisation, and that is your moment. 'As a matter of fact, Lord so-and-so, I've been thinking that we ought to have a brief word on ...' Brilliant; a new contact; put it in the address book.

There is no stronger way of building a career than 'working the corridors'.

Richard Humphreys (serial Chairman)

You can expand on this by dropping in on anyone. Hewlett Packard used to have a useful slogan 'managing by wandering around'. It was a neat way of reminding managers that part of their job was to be around and meet people by chance as well as in formal meetings. I extended this to 'selling by wandering around', which meant using the same technique to cruise around customer premises making new, preferably high-level, contacts. 'Building your career by wandering around?' – it's not as snappy but that doesn't mean that it doesn't work.

It is basically better to be in the office at the same time as your boss. After all, they might give an interesting and potentially rewarding opportunity to someone else. So know their diaries so that you can plan your absences at times when they will not notice.

The clincher for knowing your boss's diary is that you will know when he or she is definitely far away; since there is nothing more embarrassing than being caught nosing around in someone else's files.

Idea 30 – It's not about how you play the game …

The rest of this rhyme goes, 'But who you get to take the blame.' This is the business version of the Olympic spirit. It is generally not a good idea to be closely associated with failure. Steer clear of the firing line unless there are massive brownie points for effort as opposed to achievement.

There is another way of looking at this if the cock-up is really huge. A person in charge of a substantial development project spent £50 million of his company's

---

Career clue

Short-sighted people with moderate ambitions keep detailed notes of their activities with a special section for the people who supported them on the way. The more ambitious person with their eye on the big picture does it in such a way that the record can prove that others were completely responsible if it goes wrong. Don't forget to have a shredder handy if all goes well, though. It wouldn't do for you to enable someone else to take the glory.

money on it and was, towards the end, powerless to prevent it having no impact on the business at all. The entire sum was completely wasted. Asked in to his boss's office he pre-empted the inevitable by saying that he knew he was there to be fired. 'No way', said his boss, a very aware woman. 'Now that we have spent £50 million in your learning what doesn't work, we are not about to throw that investment away.' It's a variant of 'Owe your bank £1000, it's your problem; owe it a million and it's theirs.'

Idea 31 – Choose your friends carefully

A colleague of mine tells the story of two management trainees who agreed to talk each other's work up to anyone who would listen. Five years later, they are both successful and they are still doing it. This is good technique, but be calculating in your relationships.

Remember, you have to be out of harm's way when things go wrong. Avoid the front line of a disaster area, and keep your top, i.e. senior management, cover impregnable.

Career clue from the boardroom

It is all very well being loyal and supportive to a friend who is struggling or who is incompetent and uncharismatic. But don't do it in a way that reflects on you. Give them real and meaningful support, but surreptitiously. Avoid being tarred with their brush.

Richard Humphreys (serial Chairman)

Idea 32 – Plan realistic career steps

You must know where you are going. If you are responsible for other people's careers, it would be crazy not to have a reasonable idea of where you yourself are going next. Make sure that there is no external factor that could blow your plan out of the water. A number of people are suffering from this in the technology industry. Right now, building a career on your knowledge and expertise in analogue communication is not good for business. The people with their eye in, changed to jobs in the development of digital communication some time ago.

Idea 33 – Appraise yourself well

Whilst it is good advice for you to take on all the training, away days, conferences and consultations that you are offered, despite their apparent futility; just think how it would be if these inputs into your career were specifically relevant and directional. Preparation before entering an appraisal can make all the difference. No-one is as good as you at knowing what skills you need; so help your boss along by working that out before the appraisal interview.

   Now get yourself ready and in the right frame of mind by asking yourself these questions:

Career clue from the boardroom

Always take every opportunity offered to receive training. Give careful thought to your training needs before any appraisal interview.

George Paul (Chairman, Norwich Union)

- What value have you added to your job?
- Where is it that you would like to go?
- What do you need to do to get there?
- Why should your boss support these plans? (What's in it for him/her?)

Answering these questions before an appraisal interview will mean that the time will be more beneficial to both you and your employer. Remember, this is your career; not your organisation's. Take ownership of that career and impress your boss with your motivation and determination. Nobody likes a 'yes' man any more than a 'no' man. An employee with a clear idea of their career strategy is much more impressive than someone who agrees to whatever is suggested with no proposals of his or her own.

Whilst your career is your own, remember also that you are a team player in an organisation with its own aims and strategies. It is an entity in its own right and this must be reflected in the way you express yourself during an appraisal interview. That is why the question 'why should your boss support these plans?' is so important. You need to be able to prove that you are a valuable asset to the organisation and that by investing in you, you will become even more valuable. Start from the very top. What words can you use that link your activities with the fundamental vision or mission of the organisation you work for? Then come down through the division and eventually to your boss.

Another key thing to remember when entering an appraisal is that the person interviewing you is not an unidentifiable member of the corporate zoo; they are in fact a person with their own ambitions and career plans. Be sensitive to this. Do not alienate your boss by appearing to be more ambitious, more clued up, more prepared to succeed than them (even if it's true). What you are trying to do is to get your boss to adopt your plan, which you present subtly and sensitively, because he or she can see how it is going to make him or her look good. You do not need to ram this down their throats; they can work it out.

A little flattery can go a long way. If you're feeling particularly outrageous, you could even suggest that one day you hope to attain the giddy heights of responsibility that your boss has (although this one takes a firm jaw, a straight face and a very sincere stance to get away with it). See *don't lie on your CV Idea 22*.

Recognise that normal interview techniques are suitable in an appraisal situation. You know the theory that a person interviewing makes up their mind in the first few seconds of a candidate walking through the door. This is why we polish our shoes, comb our hair and leave the cork in the bottle the previous night. Let your appraisal interview be no different. If you take the interview seriously, you and your career plans are more likely to be taken seriously. Body language, presentation and thorough preparation are what count.

You may already have a job purpose statement agreed with your employer. If not, this is an easy way to impress and will help you to get a clear picture of who you are in the organisation and what your job is. If you already have a job purpose statement, expanding on this to include your career aspirations could be an effective means of communication.

Here are some tips for a job purpose statement from *The Appraisal Checklist* by Brian Watling (Pitman, 1995):

- The statement should be short – one or two sentences will do.
- The statement should say why the job exists.
- The statement should be specific to the job being described.
- The statement must tie in with the mission statement.

Idea 34 – Find out some new facts or statistics

Left to themselves, companies ossify. Without alert managers, all organisations would fail to realise that the world in which they are operating is changing. And it is difficult to be sure what changes in the environment will have an impact on your particular organisation. This makes the gathering and proclaiming of new facts or sta tistics a fertile ground for standing out in the crowd. The aim here is to draw the attention of management to new information that might have an impact in the long term. This is an area for lateral thinking. Remember we are talking about the long term so, if your facts and trends fail to deliver the impact you predict, that will not be known for some time and you will be long gone further up the ladder.

If you do not do it now, set aside at least fifteen minutes of every day to read relevant parts of published material; you will find this invaluable in presenting yourself. If you read technical papers or even just the dailies, you will start to detect new and useful facts at an early stage. A rich vein for this type of information is the technical section. Technological change over the last ten years has rendered unnecessary hundreds of skills that were carried out by hand. When, for example, did you last see someone literally cutting and pasting a newsletter?

Send notes to appropriate people quoting sources of information such as the *Harvard Gazette* that no one is likely to have read. The conclusion that you draw from the information must give senior managers food for thought. You must lead them to some clear conclusions showing problems, preferably catastrophic ones, or opportunities, preferably big ones, in the future. The area of demographics is another dead cert. Grey people buying power, the growth of old retired people, the death rate in Russia and so on. I advocate strongly the use of real facts in this regard, but if you have to make them up, make sure it is not remotely possible to challenge them.

Career clue from the boardroom

Study your subject well; observe carefully your customer requirements; strive mightily to fulfil that customer need and work hard and diligently at all times.

Sir George Bull (Chairman, J Sainsbury)

The Internet companies of today are building huge share valuations on exactly this principle. In ten years' time there will be x billion people on the Internet, doing $y\%$ of their purchasing of food and wine online. The food and drink market will be worth z trillion in ten years' time and we will have 10% of that market making a profit margin of 20%. Discount that figure back to today, and you have a company value of billions before you've even billed a customer let alone turned a profit.

If all else fails, there is always Health and Safety and regulation. Find out what the trends are in these, and predict the impact on your organisation.

Gather new facts and statistics as often as seems sensible, given that you are also overperforming in your day-to-day function, and you will almost certainly at some point do your organisation a big favour. It would have ossified in that area if you had not warned it; organisations don't spot trends.

Health warning

Do not pull the facts and statistics stunt too often. Some people send off two notes a week. This is a mistake – you are trying to build a reputation as a person with their finger on the pulse, not as a crashing bore.

Four Greatest Ideas for Impressing the Management Panel

Introduction

Many organisations have put in place a hurdle that all potential managers, from whatever part of the business, have to jump if they are to move into management at all. This is not an interview for a specific job, but a check by people, some of whom will not know you, that you have what it takes to start on the first rung of the corporate ladder. Some companies repeat the process further up the organisation. You need to pass such panels first time and preferably easily and unanimously. It is extraordinary how the results of these affairs leak out, and failing the first time will

---

Career clue from the boardroom

Looking back on my own career I think the one thing that perhaps helped me was the breadth of my reading about the oil industry and overall economic matters in addition, of course, to being up to speed in the depth of knowledge to do the job of the moment.

Perhaps it helped that I was an economist and had an interest in reading as widely as possible; and indeed the whole subject of economics is one where at the time of my taking my original degree the macro rather than the micro was the main area of discussion and debate.

Perhaps this only means that to get on in life you have to be someone of whom it cannot be said, 'He or she cannot see the wood for the trees.'

Sir Peter Walters (Chairman, SmithKline Beecham)

be remembered as will your being on the borderline. For this interview you need to be able to display good knowledge of what management is generally about *Idea 36*, and demonstrate your knowledge of the big picture *Idea 38*. First of all, as you would expect, you must prepare well *Idea 35*.

Idea 35 – Judge your judges judiciously

This is a tricky audience because it is a mixed one. There will be a representative from human resources (HR) as well as line managers who will include the level you will be working for and probably at least one level above that. This means you have to display knowledge of the rules and regulations to HR, and a strong hint of entrepreneurial flair to the latter. Make sure you know who the people are, not only their positions but also their personal character and circumstances.

Career case in point

A manager who had just been on a management panel told me of one statement a candidate made that was perfectly fair in most circumstances but went down badly. Asked for his strengths, he included the fact of his stable and happy home life. Fair enough. He then went on about it, finishing with the peroration, 'Indeed without Margaret I think it would be much more difficult for me to work effectively and without stress.' My informant pointed out that on the panel were one woman on her third husband, one man who had replaced his wife with a person who was until recently his secretary, and one manager whose rather messy divorce was even at that time getting an occasional mention in the *News of the World*. What he said was fine, he just said it to the wrong people.

As part of your preparation speak to a wider section of people than just your boss. Whilst it is true that he or she will be helpful, their experience of these matters could be very out of date. Better to include speaking to people who have recently passed a panel, and of course, if you can find one willing to help, someone who has recently failed. Make sure that in the interview you display the preparation you have done that puts you ahead of the crowd.

When you are in there, try to make the panel speak, and then listen to what they say. All the clues will be there. You will probably fail in this with the human resources person who knows when in interviews to hold his or her tongue, but the line managers will often respond, particularly if they have already listened to a number of enthusiastic talkers.

However, there is no right and wrong way of handling the management panel, and you may like to think of doing it in an original way. I know someone who decided to make a presentation though it was not a requirement. It went well, though, and he passed with flying colours.

Idea 36 – Be able to give a simple explanation of what management is

Don't spend too much time on your past record. They know you have done well and they are testing you for your next job, not your last one. At some point you will need to show that you have thought about the job of a manager. Remember KISS (*keep it simple, stupid*). And get the level right, a mixture of pragmatic efficiency and wide thinking talent.

- Managers are there to enable their people to give of their best.
- They are effective implementers of corporate and divisional strategy. They are always able to connect their activities with the bigger picture.

- As well as implementing it, they have a role in influencing high-level strategy. First line managers are the voice of their people, markets and suppliers. They see the changes day to day and are in the best position to question or suggest alterations to the way the organisation goes about its affairs.
- Managers are a skilled resource to their team. They must add value when they are in action helping the team. When a sales manager goes to see a customer, or a purchasing manager to a supplier, for example, the plan must make them do or say something that could not be done or said by the team member. A good example is when a production manager visits a supplier and introduces the topic of the environment and other green issues.
- Managers know how the organisation works, and can thus add to the efficiency and productivity of their team.

Idea 37 – Of course I can manage

The part of the manager's job that a lot of people find difficult, at least at first, is their role in man management. They have probably already got some experience in team leadership, particularly if they have been involved in projects. But when the project team have performance or personal problems, they have been required to refer these to the person's line manager. Think about motivation, *Idea 77* might help, and treating people as individuals.

Here is an area where people at the management panel slip up. They are asked what they would do if they found that one of their people was not performing. Know the rules; so don't jump in with 'Well, sack them.' But show that having exhausted the procedures and training opportunities, you will have the authority and assertiveness to get both yourself and your team member out of a bad situation. In this regard you may want to say that you have to be careful not to spend too much time with such people since that can have an impact on the whole team's performance. See *don't fall in the tailender time trap Idea 49*, but be careful of the Human Resources person with this one – know the rules.

Show that you are looking forward to the challenges of man management, and use any experience of doing it you have picked up along the way.

Idea 38 – Be a dedicated follower of fashion

The business world is a world of fashion. Management principles come and management principles go, but the careerist is forever. Sometimes ideas last for a decade or so. The eighties was the decade of 'diversification' and then in the nineties we all scuttled back to 'core businesses'. You should know what the flavour of the month is when you attend the panel. Don't be too clever, some of the panel members may not know what you are talking about, in which case they may resort to saying that it is management speak, and not practical. In this regard 'holistic' is dangerous and 'e-synchronous supply chain' only for those who can really explain it simply with references to examples from their organisation.

At the moment of writing 'globalisation' and 'grand globalisation' are dead safe. My antennae tell me that 'empowerment' is slipping and being replaced by 'manage not as a policeman but as a coach and mentor.' 'Synergy' is everywhere, 'continuous improvement' is safe but dull, while 'strategic innovation' is the coming thing. Strategic innovation is easy enough if you explain the shrinking timescales most industries have to effect changes. In the steel industry, strategic innovation may be every twenty years, in the software industry you may have to review strategy every six months. See *if you want to get ahead, get a strategy Idea 40*, and *now implement your strategy Idea 41*.

Keep it very practical; the panel is looking for people who are good at making things happen before it looks for great thinkers.

Seven Greatest Ideas for Leading a Team to Success

Introduction

OK, so you made it over the first hurdle and joined the ranks of management. Your progress from here depends on how you actually perform and how senior managers think you perform. The latter is probably the more important, but the former gives you a good starting point. You have now to deal with concepts that, up until now, you have merely criticised others for failing at. This includes *if you want to get ahead get a strategy Idea 40. Implementing a strategy Idea 41* involves change. Change can involve pain. Use *the rule of 20% Idea 44* to get your forces behind you to minimise the pain and maximise the chances of success.

Idea 39 – Understand how markets value companies

Before you set out on the rocky road to a strategic plan, make sure that you are thoroughly familiar with how shareholders value companies. This may seem unnecessary at lower levels in the organisation, but your bit of the organisation is part of the whole.

Don't let anyone tell you otherwise – the value of a company is based on the dividend stream it pays to shareholders now and in the future. At the moment a company could be paying no dividends at all and still have a high value. But that value still stems from the fact that the company, or a successor company will pay out annual dividends to its shareholders.

To pay a higher dividend, you need higher profits and, of course, you need the cash to make the payment. Your strategy must in some way pay attention to those two requirements. If it does not make money and generate cash at some point in the implementation, it is not aimed at the heart of the company's purpose.

Investors are aware of the profits that the company made last year. That existing position is given by the yield, which is a comparison of the dividend paid last year with the value of a share. They then take a view on the management and their likelihood of being successful in implementing their plans for the future. This expectation of future dividends is encapsulated in the other interesting ratio from an investor's point of view, called the *price earnings ratio* (P/E) or the *multiple*. It simply records the market value of a share as a multiple of the company's earnings per share. If last year's earnings were £1 million in total and there are 1 million shares issued, then the earnings per share will be £1. If the investors who are studying the likely future performance of the company are paying £20 for a share, then the P/E is 20. It gives us the market's view of the future prospects of the company.

Everyone uses the historic earnings as the basis for the P/E because that is the only solid number that everybody has. If investors have taken an optimistic view of the likely growth prospects of the company, the P/E will be much higher than if they regard the prospects for growth as slow.

Look at the P/E of your organisation and, as you approach your strategic plan, be aware that the profits you plan and forecast must bear good comparison with the overall P/E. If you are in the core business of your organisation and, for example, the P/E is 12, then make sure that the overall budget you plan at the end of the planning process shows a return on investment of at least 12%. There is more of this in planning a project *Idea 76*.

Idea 40 – If you want to get ahead, get a strategy

The word *strategy* is possibly the most ill-used piece of management speak in the business. You will frequently hear middle managers complaining that their board of directors does not have a strategy. This is normally not the case. Their strategy may be wrong, their strategy may need to change to react to events, but they do have a strategy. Maybe middle management have not been told about it or maybe middle management has misunderstood it. It is, in fact, the definition of the board that they plan strategy, so you need a reputation as a strategic thinker to get to the top.

Come down a few levels to team leaders in whatever department, and the accusation 'They do not have a strategy' starts to look truer. It is difficult for team leaders to have an up to date strategy, particularly in organisations that do not give concrete guidelines on what a strategy is and how, and most importantly when, to review it. Difficulties abound:

- It is difficult for a team leader to build a strategy because it takes time.
- It is difficult because short-term pressures stop the team getting on with the job of creating a strategy and, even if the team does, it frequently ignores the strategy whenever a customer or other significant pressure blows it off course.
- Your best strategy may be impossible because other parts of the business will not change to suit you.
- Building a team strategy needs consensus, which means that some team members are going to have to compromise over what they see as the best way ahead.

So, if it's difficult, it must be an area where the smart manager can build some career points. Put simply, you need to build a strategy with your team, agree it with all your main stakeholders or interested parties including your customers, and flaunt it. Anyone with an interest in, or a part to play in, or has an impact on your strategy is known as a stakeholder. Although it comes later in the piece, I must mention communication here because it goes through every phase of strategy building. Know who your key stakeholders are and give them good, continuous and well-targeted information at the right time.

The first skill involved is the ability to balance short-term thinking with long-term planning. Put it in your schedule. Make regular time to review your long-term prospects. You do not have much time; you needed a strategy yesterday. And, who knows, you may need a new one tomorrow. The time span between reviews depends on the business you are in and on external events such as competitive activity. The steel industry can afford to put in place a strategy and leave it more or less undisturbed for many years. The software industry may need to carry out major reviews of strategy twice a year. If one of your customers is taken over, or two of your competitors merge, you may need to review your strategy and announce it all within one day.

Here is some step by step advice for agreeing a team strategy. Start from what a strategy is not:

- the annual budgeting round – don't mistake this for strategy – we will come to budgeting activities when the rest of the strategy is well worked out;
- a large book of management speak containing mission statements of 400 words that attempt to cover all the aspirations of the management team without pausing for breath – here is one of these at board level:

> *Our strategic intent is to strive for leadership in the most attractive global communications segments through speed in anticipating and fulfilling evolving customer needs, quality in products and processes, as well as openness with people and to new ideas and solutions. Based on our resources including technological know-how, market position and continuous building of competencies, we are well positioned to achieve our future goals.*

'Yes but what are you going to do?', you want to scream. When I read a mission statement like that, I cannot help thinking of the old limerick:

There was a young man from Milan,
Whose limericks never would scan,
When his friends asked him why,
He said with a sigh,
'It's because I always try to put as many words into the last line as I possibly
    can.'

Back to what a strategy is not:

- a document produced by a staff function, carried around only by the same people, who use it solely to demonstrate that what the line departments are doing is against the strategy; nor
- a matrix of numbers produced once a year and left on the shelf until such time as it is due for review.

Right, keep it simple, what is it? A strategy is a plan of what you are going to sell to what markets and how you are going to do that. The strategic plan allows everyone to know how they should do their jobs, what the boundaries are and how the team leader will appraise any suggestions for doing new things. It is the team leader's job to bring focus to the team's work and make sure that the results are actionable rather than business-school babble.

Start from the selling idea. Whether or not your customer is internal or external to your organisation, you have a customer. What is a customer? – someone who buys your products and services. A group of customers is called a market, so a strategy looks at segments called product markets. The idea here is that you do not have a product if there is no market, and there is no market if you do not have a product. Think in product markets rather than products and markets, and you are on the way to having a strategy.

Here is a nine-step way for your team to build and agree a strategy in a reasonably short time – say two days' teamwork over four weeks, with everyone doing about two man days of preparatory work in the same time period.

Strategic analysis

1   First work out where you are now and what is going to happen in your world in the future. Make a list of every trend or fact that will have an impact on what you are going to do. Trends are the most important part of this. Which way are your products and services developing? What are your market's requirements over the next two years? You may have to take into consideration economic, legal and political trends. You will certainly have to think about technological changes and their potential impact on your plan. Now get the team to find out the facts behind every trend on the list.

2   Analyse your customers and your competitors. Write down the buying criteria that your customers use to decide whether to buy from you or the competition. This gives you what they think is important. Now write against each of the criteria what the customer would ideally like. If, for example, *ease of use* is an

---

Career case in point

The chairman of a South East brewery, when presented with some ideas for the use of e-commerce in 1999 said, 'All this Internet publicity is a flash in the pan. It's just kids' stuff. E-commerce will never catch on in business.'

Mmm, I hope someone improves his or her career by getting through to him.

important criterion, then the ideal the customer might use is *requires no special off-the-job training*. Neither you nor your competitors may be able to achieve the customer's ideal, but if you know what it is, you have an aiming point. As objectively as you can, measure yourself and your competitors against this customer ideal. This will give you a series of threats, where your competitor is ahead, and opportunities where you can see you have an advantage.

3   Now examine your internal capabilities. Look at your business processes, your information systems and your facilities and equipment. Finally look at the team and assess its skills and experience. This step will give you a list of areas where you need to make improvements.

4   Summarise the analysis using the SWOT analysis technique. Simply group all the key issues into the headings *strengths*, *weaknesses*, *opportunities* and *threats*. Take some time to check your analysis with other stakeholders like your boss and your customers. You are now ready to make a plan.

Making the plan

5   Define your overall purpose. Why does your team exist? Keep it simple and clear. For example, you are not here to 'exploit our knowledge of the food industry'; you are here to 'sell bulk food and specialist foods to the European market (predominantly the UK) in the next two years.' Even this simple statement may take time to agree. Someone is bound to object that if that is the purpose, what is going to happen to the home delivery service and so on. But once it is agreed, you have the first brick in the wall of strategy.

6   Now look for your competitive advantage. Once again this is a brief statement of why customers have bought and will buy from you rather than anyone else. If your customer is an internal one, then do not forget that they too have choice. Make sure that your competitive advantage of being in the same company holds water. There are a lot of outsourced computer departments wishing their strat-

egy had included thinking about that. If you honestly cannot think of your competitive advantage, ask your customer. You should in any case check it over with the customer in a sensitive way.

7   Set boundaries. A strategy is not only about what you are going to do, it is also about what you are not going to do. Write it down and get everyone to agree to it. Tricky if it means ruling out some pet projects, or if you put one customer requirement outside the boundary when the salesman who deals with that customer is pushing hard for its inclusion.

8   Here comes the crunch. Choose the areas of emphasis in terms of product markets. Once you know this emphasis, you will be able to allocate resources accordingly. Take a matrix and write your product groups down the left hand side, and your market groups across the top. Into each cell in the matrix put what the current emphasis is, either high, medium or low, and what your future emphasis will be. You may get some surprises here, like finding that a major area of resource is actually working in a product market that is fast declining. All good stuff, and your strategy is taking shape.

9   From this emphasis document, or activity matrix, you should be able to produce an overview of the budget. What value of sales should you strive for, what costs will you incur and therefore, what profit should you expect? Incidentally, this overview should make the filling in of the annual budgeting forms very straightforward.

Throughout the process be prepared to question and challenge accepted norms. The really upwardly mobile fight tooth and nail before acknowledging that something the company is doing wrong cannot be changed. But watch the politics. It is a tough call, but you have to make a judgement on whether entrenched views held by your bosses can be challenged by you at this time. But in my experience, and the experience of those I talked to about this book, the safety-first acquiescence path is so much the easier to contemplate, that most people err on that side rather than

---

Career case in point

The powerful people behind Marks and Spencer over the last five years are a good case in point. Two of their strategies, the sourcing strategy and the marketing strategy, failed to keep up with events. Whilst companies like Adidas were combating the threat of bankruptcy by recognising the inevitability of using overseas suppliers, M&S doggedly pushed on with their 'Buy British' strategy.

Similarly they clung to their 'No Advertising' strategy until their market share had declined disastrously and the bad PR avalanche had more than halved the share price and, would you believe it, made them vulnerable to takeover. Eventual realisation was too late and the top directors lost their jobs.

---

taking the risk of becoming known as a doubter, or worse a troublemaker. *Courage, mon brave*, nobody said life was easy.

Prepare to shine. You have a strategy and, to prove it, it is written down. Tell people about it, partly because you are trying to build your career and partly because you want to influence others towards your way of thinking. Make presentations. Sell your methodology to others so that you become the source of the company-wide strategic planning system. Finally exploit the fact that you now know the reality behind building a strategy; so when someone complains that the board does not have a strategy, confidently ask him or her to explain, 'What exactly do you mean by a strategy?' You will be amazed how many cannot say, or give you a line from a limerick.

Idea 41 – Now implement your strategy

A military man once observed, 'No strategic plan ever survived contact with the enemy', and so it is in business. No strategic plan ever survived unscathed in the market place. Prepare to implement and change your strategy – this is the tough bit. You need a reputation as a strategic thinker, and you do that by building a strategy, but real credibility in this area comes from making it happen. The key is KISS (*keep it simple, stupid*), and remember Sir John Collins' advice, 'Perform as advertised'.

Define change projects

You will have discovered in setting the strategy many gaps and problems in the way you do things now. A good SWOT analysis will point at the areas for improvement. They may be legion, so you will have to prioritise them. Once again a major benefit of implementing a strategy is that you decide what you are not going to improve, as well as where you are going to take action. Boil the prioritised list down to a manageable size of five or six issues. Call each of these a change project and you should manage them just like that – as projects. Set objectives for the change and a timescale for it to occur. Put someone in charge of it and use your leadership skills to keep momentum behind the change projects even when day-to-day events threaten to swamp any longer-term thinking.

Learn from experience

Implementing change projects is an area bogged down in management speak. It is also an area where your humility needs to shine through. Ask for help. Somewhere in your organisation someone has done something like it before. Learn from them. You do not need to quote them as the source, and you will do things differently to

---

Career case in point

In one large company a lot of change was necessary in order to move its culture from a state-owned monopoly to a competitive business. Management produced a screed of initiatives aimed at changing how everyone went about doing their jobs. The trouble was that there were so many that they were never properly followed through. A lot of work would be done in a staff function, but what actually happened in the field was rarely touched. The wags on the shop floor gave the tidal wave of initiatives the acronym BOHICA (*bend over, here it comes again*).

---

avoid charges of imitation, but make sure you have learned the lessons from the past before setting off on a change project with little chance of success.

Write your bible

So, you have a series of change projects with objectives and timescales. Now draw up the strategy 'bible'. This is a folder containing one page, if possible, describing each change project. On it will be the milestones you will use to check that the project is on track, the actions in a sensible level of detail, the owner of each action and milestone, and the time by which it needs to be complete. Keep it simple so that monitoring the plan is straightforward.

Check the plan for risk

You are nearly ready to implement the strategy. But check it first for risks. You do not want to give publicity to a strategy that is eventually written off as BOHICA. Look for the down side. What could go wrong? What will you do if it does go wrong? Is there any contingency plan you can put in place to mitigate the risks, and so on? If any of your colleagues are genuine friends, or if any of your friends are competent, ask them to add their views to this part of the planning process. If you can defend it against them, you have a copper-bottomed winner. Finally check it for risks not from the company's point of view but, more to the point, from that of your career.

Review your operational targets

Now think about the linkage between a new strategy and operations. The new strategy should put you in a position where your results will improve. The changes you are making will result in higher sales or profit and improve customer satisfaction. This is your best lever for obtaining the other implication of the new plan – more resources. It is a well-known fact of business life that if any person asks to speak to their boss, it is because they want more resources in some way. Your new strategy gives you the opportunity to do this in a much more logical way than perhaps your colleagues are using. The logic you use is as follows: I will give you these improved operational results if you give me this increase in resources. Take care. Managers, particularly I find, sales managers, are brilliant at agreeing to one side of your proposition but not the other. 'I like the results – we'll have them – but you can't have the resources.' Make the linkage logical and absolute, or they will at best water down the resources on offer and at worst just up your operational targets.

Review roles and responsibilities

The one certainty of reviewing and changing your strategy is that people's jobs will change. Agree these changes with them and alter the reward scheme if possible. Many a bright shiny new strategy has faltered on the simple proposition that the incentive scheme supports the old one.

If people need training, invest the company's money in it. Do not forget that when you are investing money in your people's training, you are also investing it in your own career. Offering training allows you to reward success, build personal loyalty and demonstrate that your part of the business is well enough under control that you can release staff for self-development.

Communicate the strategy

OK, it's time to go public. Whether or not you actually manage the strategy right through its implementation, make sure you get the kudos for its creation by telling everyone about it. Well, not everyone, but anyone who needs to know and is in some major or minor way impacted by the changes you are making. It is a rule of life that if someone's job is affected by a change in strategy, they can stop it dead. But don't send everyone the whole plan. The warehouseman in Newbury does not need to see the whole illustrated document if the only thing it means to him is that his hours have changed from starting at 8.30 to starting at 8.00. Do a management summary, take out appropriate extracts for different individuals and use presentations, if you are any good at them, but sparingly. You should by now have the agreement of all the key people to your plan; so tell people what is going to happen in order to make it more likely that it will happen. A word of caution: make sure that people see the plan in the order that suits your personal interests. Be especially careful with middle managers who may take the plan to higher levels with a heavy implication that they had influence on the work. Don't let them take credit for good ideas that should make *you* a star.

Monitor the implementation

The way you have documented the plan should make this aspect relatively easy. Use a green, amber and red system in your and your people's reports. Against each operational target or each milestone in a change project, ask the people responsible to report on at least a monthly basis. Your meeting agenda then consists of taking the red issues first and the amber ones second. Assuming that most of the plan is at green, review meetings will be focused and of reasonable length.

Then change it all again

The reality of strategic thinking and planning is that it never stops. Harold Macmillan, when asked what his biggest problems were, said 'Events, dear boy. Events.' How very true. Keep checking the strategy to see if it is still relevant and feasible. Competitors come up with new ideas, technology changes, and people leave one job for another. All of these and myriad more events require you to make changes to even the greatest strategy of all time.

Remember you want a reputation as a strategic thinker in order to get to the top, but don't stay around too long – this events business is a bastard.

Idea 42 – Remember that your underpants are inside your tights

You are not Superman. Take a cold hard look at the new strategy and implementation plan, and ask yourself, 'Can I do this?' If you have followed a logical process you will have produced the best plan. It means change and new challenges. Suppose it were to include the need for you to go scuba diving. Would you just get hold of the equipment and jump straight in? No, you would make sure you went to a reputable trainer and learnt how to swim underwater safely.

So it is with implementing strategy. Do you have the skills to carry it through? It probably needs an amount of *project management Ideas 75–78*. It may test your knowledge of financial techniques or take you into new areas of people management. You almost certainly do not have all the knowledge you need at hand or in your head. Are your computer skills up to it, or are you going to waste time by not exploiting technology to its optimum? Since you are building a career, the strategy will certainly take you into conversations with a higher level of management than you have dealt with before. (If it doesn't, dummy, go back and rewrite that bit.) Are you confident you can deal with them? And so on.

If you cannot do something, admit it. It is much better to say you cannot do it. This makes you learn, adds to your skills and takes out some of the risk of non-performance. Everyone I have spoken to in researching this book emphasises putting yourself continuously into situations where you can learn.

Idea 43 – And so are your people's

If you find it difficult to admit that you cannot do something your people will as well. Encourage them to talk about those parts of the strategy where they are less confident that they know what to do or know they cannot do. Then you can help them, or rearrange the plan to take that task away from them. I have often been in conference rooms where a good strategy has been thrashed out, but it has been obvious that the current team has not the skills to implement it. I have pointed this out and the team has made some modifications or made plans for self-development. I have even sat with senior managers brought in for the final presentation of the plan, and when the team has left the room they have turned to me and said 'Great plan, Ken, but that lot can't do it.' It begs the question, 'Why are you letting them try?'

Idea 44 – Rule of 20%

Managing change can be a depressing business but there is hope in this rule. There has been research in production and other environments to support a rule of thumb that I have found to be true practically. If you have to manage a change process, you need *agents of change* to support you. Agents of change are people who fundamentally agree with the need for change and have the will to go through the process themselves. I assisted with the production of strategic plans for all the power stations of a European Electricity Supply Company that was preparing to become a private company, having belonged to the state all its life.

Senior management knew that there would be fierce resistance to the changes that had to be made, and they decided to include the whole management team of each power station in planning the new strategy *Idea 40*. This gave us rather large teams of up to twenty people, but seemed the right way to go. The resistance differed from station to station, and a pattern emerged. In the more progressive stations where, say, 50% of the team could be regarded as agents of change either before the planning session or after it, we could already see the first signs of successful change. If at the planning session there were 20%, it was harder work but it could be made to happen. Below that, it looked and turned out to be hopeless. And, of course there was one where no agent of change appeared, not even the station manager, and we failed there. So the rule of 20% is a practical one.

So, before you start out to implement change, make sure you can name the agents of change and that their number obeys this rule. Caucus with them if you have to, and explain their role in helping you. If you break up into work groups or task forces either in the planning or implementation phase, seed them in amongst the laggards. Incidentally if you do not take charge of the groupings, the agents of change will work together and you will lose their contribution to converting the non-believers. So when you hear a depressed manager talking about the daunting task of getting a hundred managers to change the way they work, ask him how many will be supportive to begin with. If there is more than 20%, tell him of the rule and encourage him to go for it. If it is less than that number, just leave him or her, politely, to get on with it. Don't get involved, or you will find that depression is contagious.

Idea 45 – Be the director of a string quartet, not a play

In his autobiography *Writing Home*, the playwright Alan Bennett gives an insight into different attitudes amongst team members. He differentiates musicians from actors. In the first case:

> *Striking about the musicians is their total absence of self-importance.*

He describes how the musicians play a piece and then discuss amongst themselves as to how it might be improved. They make suggestions for each other directly, not via the director. Anyone is invited to comment, their views noted and in some cases adopted when they repeat the piece. According to Bennett this would be impossible with actors.

> *No actor would tolerate a fellow performer who ventured to comment on what he or she is doing – comment of that sort coming solely from the director, and even then it has to be carefully packaged and seasoned with plenty of love and appreciation.*

This is just what it is in business. In most teams the egos of the individuals get in the way of sharing suggestions. There are exceptions and they tend to be successful people. Watch out for them. They encourage openness and constructive criticism of everyone, by everyone. They tend to be very laid back, good listeners and very understanding of people's problems. When they are team members, they are terrific allies of the team leader and still liked by their colleagues in the team. When they are team leaders they bring the best out of people continuously. They don't manage everyone in the same way, though: some of the team they can encourage to be musicians, and some will always be actors.

Four Greatest Ideas for
Standing Out in the More Senior Crowd

Introduction

Once you have made it to first and second line management, the crowd has thinned out a bit – that's the good news. The bad news is that the real no-hopers have mostly disappeared and standing out in the smaller crowd is a bit more difficult. All the competition has, at some point, impressed senior people with their achievements or just their *bonhomie* and charisma. The four ideas here, therefore, concentrate on performance and adding value to the organisation, although *put up a paper Idea 48* has got a lot of froth and bubble about it.

Idea 46 – Don't come to me with your problems

There is nothing more frustrating for a manager than to be the recipient continuously of information that turns out to be a problem. It may come as a surprise to a lot of people but their managers do not automatically know what to do in all circumstances. It happens at all levels. I have known chairmen and other senior managers still showing frustration at the way people present them with information.

There are the three ways of telling your boss that there is a problem:

- Take the piece of information, whether it is a competitor that has brought out a new product or a big customer who has gone bust, to your boss and wait for him or her to give you instructions for what needs to be done either immediately or in due course.

- Analyse your company's position in the light of the information. A very good way of doing this is to use simple SWOT analysis – strengths, weaknesses, opportunities and threats. What are the strengths that your company could use to combat the turn of events? What are the weaknesses that will make an effective response difficult? What opportunities does the new situation offer your company, and what are threats to performance if nothing is done? This is a much preferable approach to your boss than the first. It saves them the time to think the analysis through and makes it easier to make a decision. Watch your timing on this. If the problem is that the competitor has brought out a new product, you probably have more time to weigh up the situation than if the big customer has gone bust. Don't over-analyse and tell your boss too late. Having said that, more people err on the side of going in too quickly, where more preparation would have been useful, than go in too late.
- Using the SWOT analysis, come to a conclusion. Think through a well structured line of reasoning that supports your recommendation, and present the solution rather than the problem

Most people take the first approach, some the second but only a few the third. If you think about it from the point of view of the manager whose daily lot it is to receive a continuous stream of information about problems, you will see how the solution presenters really do stand out in the crowd.

The help that your 'solutions not problems' approach gives to your boss does have a downside. He or she may disagree with your solution, or by chance know a much better one from experience. But if you never make a mistake you are not trying to add value. Which brings us to the next idea.

Idea 47 – Take responsibility for your own actions

When asked what type of person she wanted to employ, a middle manager responded:

The corporate world is made up of two types of person, those who play the game and those who watch it. You can tell them by what makes them feel good. The watcher goes home fulfilled if they have worked hard and used their skills. They have performed their tasks. The players only feel good if they have accomplished something. They finish things. They don't pass the buck. Funnily enough it is the players who make most mistakes. The watchers can't, because if you are not playing, you can't lose. Mind you, you can't win either.

Career clue from the boardroom

John Newbern put it as succinctly, but in three groups, 'Those who make things happen, those who watch things happen and those who ask, 'What happened?''

Idea 48 – Put up a paper

At any point in the chaos that describes your organisation, there can come an opportunity for you to make a sensible suggestion, which, if good enough, could make your star shine. Be continuously on the look-out. There will be a product feature kept too long to be competitive, a business process that reflects how things were some time ago, or an opportunity for using technology that will make a significant contribution to the effectiveness of the organisation. Other possibilities are for publicity or sponsorship. (If you know the arts or sport preferences of the chief executive, you might just stumble across a local opportunity for sponsorship. If you pull it off, you can be sure the chief executive will be there for the event.) We have already looked at making suggestions about the organisational structure that has the added possibility of identifying a new job for you: *abolish your job Idea 6* and *create a new post Idea 7*.

First make sure that your idea is in an area where the issues are being discussed at least two levels above you, not the specific issues of your paper but related. Now put up a paper.

Keep it brief, simple and in their terms *Idea 2*. Use the same formula for the document as discussed in *present yourself well Idea 27*:

Career clue

This is an example of perhaps the shortest proposal document ever. A European car manufacturer decided to double its marketing and advertising budgets, and mounted a search for whom they should spend it with. They selected six advertising agencies and gave them a detailed brief and six weeks to perfect their presentations. Other agencies tried to gatecrash the shortlist with no success, until through a lucky break a seventh agency, much smaller than the original six, managed to catch the eye of the advertiser's team. There was one snag – only five days including a weekend to go before the presentations.

The other six agencies had their creative brainwaves early on and had had weeks to turn over every wheel nut in the industry and dissect every available statistic. Each gave presentations that went on beyond the allotted two hours – possibly their big mistake. Each handed over, modestly but proudly, a documented record of all their wisdom, from the inside finger measurement of driving gloves in different parts of the country, to moody scenarios for brilliantly lit *oeuvres d'art* for ice driving, shot through blue vaselined lenses. Not one proposal contained fewer than sixty lovingly crafted pages.

The seventh agency had no choice – one creative idea, one sign off line and one handout to remind the prospective client of their hour upon the stage. It was a postcard. A seminal still from the suggested commercial, and on the other side 'the' line from the television ad., and the agency name. They got the account the following day, awarded with reciprocal style. Expecting bad news, the agency team was called in by the client. 'Your handout was very comprehensive, but it did not answer one question – would you like a glass of champagne?'

Richard Humphreys (serial Chairman)

- scope of the paper showing the areas covered;
- background showing what you have done to get to this point;
- problem or opportunity in their terms;
- basis of decision by which they should judge your solution;
- solution, very specific;
- benefits to the organisation including what is in it for them; and
- future plan of action.

Once you have written it, try to shorten it significantly, say by half. Throw out anything except the essentials. Remember you want to have the opportunity to discuss it, so if it is too comprehensive you may have given the thing lock, stock and barrel for someone else to dine out on. Release it effectively. By effectively I mean in the way that best serves your interests. After all, it was your idea.

A good paper may help in other ways as well. There are lots of conferences out there, and lots of organisers looking for people to read papers to them. Try to find one within or without your organisation. Reading a paper anywhere abroad, for example, looks good on the CV.

Idea 49 – Don't fall in the tailender time trap

It is very interesting to ask managers which of their people they spend most time with. In the anecdotal experience of a colleague and myself, the great majority of young managers, and quite a lot of older ones, have fallen into the trap of spending an inordinate amount of time with those people in their team who are performing badly. Let's take a logical look at this. Any team will have an average distribution of performance. The bulk of the team will achieve between 90 and 100 per cent of their operational targets. The high fliers will be few in number but will achieve, on average, say 120 per cent of what was required. That leaves the tailend Charlies, the people who are not making it – say scoring in the 40s or low 50s of target.

If we talk numbers, there could be 5% of low performers, and 5% of high fliers. That leaves up to 90% of the team as good solid performers. It is the low performers themselves who set the tailend trap. They are trying to improve. They seek assistance continuously; they try to involve their manager in their work because they know that that improves their numbers and that they have lots of problems. If you fall in the trap you will give them all this assistance and use up your time. Suppose you are effective with some of them. It will only be with some of them since by definition a few will be complete no-hopers. The ones you help to improve get their performance up to what – 50–60 per cent maximum?

It is much better to spend that time with the bulk of your team, and try and get their average performance up. If you spend your time training and coaching these people, preparing tools to help with productivity and showing them exemplars of how to perform better, you may raise their average by a significant percentage. This improvement is spread across more people and your overall performance will take a big jump.

But what do you do with your low performers? This is a tough one, particularly if it is impossible or undesirable to fire them. The answer is also tough. Ignore them. Give them a strictly limited amount of your time. At best they will get the message and move on. At worst they will move on criticising you for being unhelpful. You will have covered yourself for this latter response in advance by explaining what you are doing to your boss. And if he or she is actually in the tailender time trap they could be very grateful for your help.

Four Greatest Ideas for Spending the Organisation's Money Frugally

Introduction

It is often the cry from top management that their people should spend the company's money as though it were their own. A major company, Hewlett Packard, before it broke itself up, wrote of this in the chairman's statement in the Annual Report. In 1996 he talked about the need to reduce further operating expenses. In 1997 he used quite intemperate language to say that he was sick and tired of demanding that managers curtail their expenditure. It was only in 1998, some three years since the need first became urgent, that he congratulated people on having changed the ratio of expenses to sales. If it takes a company of the quality of Hewlett Packard that length of time and that type of public statement to make it happen, it is plainly a problem. Here are three ideas with a dual purpose. Firstly they are perfectly good ideas for trading more profitably. Secondly they lead to further potential implementations of their principle.

Idea 50 – The rule of 2%

There are many reasons why a reasonable knowledge of the finance side of business is important to your career development. Don't be afraid of the detail that this brings you into. Here are two salutary tales of two middle managers with opposing views of how to manage a profit and loss account.

Sally Cranfield is an account manager at Compusell, a supplier of computer solutions, and she has a problem. Sally's job is to increase sales of computer products and services to her accounts. She has to do it profitably but the important measures she works towards are orders and deliveries or revenue. This is made more significant by the fact that the salespeople under her are targeted solely on orders. This brings her under huge pressure to make each proposal they put in front of customers as competitive as possible, particularly in terms of price.

Here is the estimated profit and loss account for a deal in which her people are involved.

	No of units	Price per unit	Total
Sales	100	10	1000
Variable costs	100	6	600
Fixed costs			300
Profit			100

The salesperson involved in the sale gives her one problem, production give her another and administration a third. The customer, she is informed by the salesperson, wants to buy from Compusell, but has a cheaper offer from a competitor. He thinks that if Sally could knock just 2% off the price per unit, the purchaser can take a case for buying from Compusell to the board. That discount plus reducing the order to only 98 units will make the customer's budget work.

The production department have had the agreement of management to a slight increase in the price of the unit; it's only 2%, but in the circumstances she cannot pass this on to the customer.

Administration has been saying for some time that there would be a slight increase in their costs due to increased charges from the IT department. It's only 2%.

Sally knows that these four changes to the proposition are all against the interests of her profit and loss account, but the numbers seem small, the customer has a lot of clout, and the sales person is going to miss his target if he does not get this order. She agrees to the changes.

Look at the actual damage this decision makes to the profit and loss account.

	No of units	Price per unit	Total
Sales	98	9.8	960.4
Variable costs	98	6.12	599.76
Fixed costs			306
Profit			54.64

Each 2% adjustment, all to Sally's disadvantage, has combined to knock nearly 46% off the profit of this deal.

Over at HAR, a recruitment consultancy, Andy McRae the new managing director is also taking a number of seemingly small decisions aimed at starting the process of re-establishing falling profitability. His executives sell a package of material to clients to keep them up to date on matters to do with employment law.

A major HAR client is likely to buy 100 of these and Andy wonders if the executive could do better. 'I want every one to sell just a few more of these,' he says to the executives 'get each client to take just 2% more copies even though we are increasing the selling price a little, by 2%.'

He buys the package from a printer/packager whom he convinces should lower the cost to HAR just a fraction, just 2%.

He had also been working for a while on the administration function and told them to find some economies, 'Every little helps,' he says, 'just knock me 2% off what you spend right now.

Andy's starting point was exactly the same as Sally's but he has made the slight adjustments in his favour.

The deal to the major client now looks like this:

	No of units	Price per unit	Total
Sales	100	10.2	1040.4
Variable costs	100	5.88	599.76
Fixed costs			294
Profit			146.64

When the 2% works in your favour, the addition to the profit is over 46%. Andy's company went from strength to strength – but they never recruited Sally.

When you think that Compusell is doing similar deals all over the world you can see the huge difference these tiny adjustments make. And that is why you need to understand the detail. You will end up making some tough decisions, but the rule of 2% could work for you starting today.

Idea 51 – Negotiate for everything

Managers who work for large corporations will complain that *the rule of 2% Idea 50* has a logical flaw. The production department of Compusell has the agreement of management to raise their price to the sales force; so how can an account manager change that and avoid paying the increased price. The answer is that in business everything is negotiable. Try it. Ring up an internal department and complain about their prices. You are, after all their customer. In Sally's case it might work if she explains that the new price makes it impossible for her to make the sale at all. Production wants to sell their products and could come to an accommodation. It may be tricky to steer such a change through the management accounting systems; but where there's a will there's a way.

Negotiating is a part of our lives; we do it all the time. In fact we do it so often, we probably do not realise that we are doing it. If you have children, you probably have already done some negotiation already today at the breakfast table. Imagine telling a child that anything at all is non-negotiable. Fat chance. You can learn a lot from watching children negotiate. They have no inhibitions, they are prepared to use the sanctions they have available to them, and they are completely devoted to the present with no thought for the future. These are all negotiating skills we lose as we grow up.

It will not surprise readers of this book to discover that the first rule of negotiation is preparation, *understand your starting point Idea 9*. Do not go into any negotiation to 'see what they are going to say'. Prepare positively. Look for reasons why the other person should see that your proposition has value rather than that you should be allowed to maintain your price. Negative preparation is a disease with commission-based sales people. Try it out. Give a salesperson the authority to give away a ten per cent discount, and every deal done from that day will have the discount deducted. The second non-surprise about negotiating is that preparation includes knowing exactly what your objectives are, *pinpoint the destination Idea 10*. Think widely. Look for objectives beyond, for example, price. What else could you get from the other party? Now put those objectives into priorities. You will have some objectives that you must achieve, some that you are going to work hard to achieve and some that would be nice to achieve. Now think of the other person's priorities in the same way. In fact think about all aspects of the person with whom you are

---

Career clue

When you negotiate, you use your own flair as well as your company's rules. Managers like people who are entrepreneurial and are aware that this sometimes involves walking over the company's normal business processes. Such entrepreneurs are regarded as good, but run the risk of upsetting others who play by the rules. Strike a balance here if you want to impress everyone.

about to negotiate. The more you understand them, the more likely you are to find a solution they will deem acceptable.

Now you get into the discussion stage. You are never going to believe it but the key to doing well at this stage is to listen, *sorry, did you say something? Idea 11*. Look at it this way. If you listen more than you talk in a negotiation it almost certainly means that you know more about the other party than they know about you. This logically leads you to a solution that suits them. You already know the solution that suits you. The opposite of listening in negotiating is interrupting. When you interrupt someone you are telling them to shut up. You are demeaning their arguments and suggesting that they cannot say anything useful to take the matter forward. If you imagine using those words instead of just interrupting, you can see that they would soon have the negotiation at loggerheads.

So you have marshalled your arguments, and both sides have laid at least some of their cards on the table. The fact that you are both still there means that you have tacitly agreed that your opening position is negotiable. You have listened for signals from the other side of where there is room for manoeuvre or compromise. At some

---

Career clue from the boardroom

My way was to plan what I wanted, try to distract the quarry by conceding generously on minor points, and hope the big ones slip through. The key is to listen first. Let them dig a hole for themselves. In one case I had planned to ask for fees of £10,000 per month, but I didn't answer the straight question of 'how much?' Eventually the client, after a preamble about how hard and competitive times were, asked us if we would mind working for a fee of 'just £20,000 a month at first' until he could justify a budget increase to his boss. Surely the best return on investment for lunch at the Groucho an adman could hope for.

Richard Humphreys (serial Chairman)

point comes the time to make a proposal. Do it sensitively and tentatively. Don't look as if you are rushing. Imagine if someone selling you something came up with a proposal to discount the price before you had even asked. You would smell a rat. The proposal will in the end become unambiguous and specific but you are looking for signals from the other side that they will find the eventual proposal acceptable. Strike a balance between a concrete offer and a flexible suggestion. A concrete offer once rejected makes the negotiation difficult and can at worst lead to deadlock. On the other hand show too much flexibility and the other side will assume that you are prepared to give in every area. You can at this stage be firm on those parts of the negotiation where you know that there will be no difficulty in their accepting. Your first proposal should be realistic, but on the high side. I have run a negotiating exercise in training events and found that there is a huge correlation between opening high and ending up with a higher than average result. Then move in small steps. Why do salespeople think that the first number in a discount is ten per cent? It's not; it's 1% or 0.5% if that makes sense. It is often useful to link parts of a proposal together. 'If you can do this, then we can do that.' Give any proposal made to you some consideration even although you may want to reject it completely. Oh, and listen to the whole of the proposition – don't interrupt.

You may at this stage see an acceptable solution as a parcel of related items. Present it as such. Give your conditions first and then the parcel including their and your concessions. Remember to give concessions reluctantly even if they actually make no difference to you, which is sometimes the case. The parcel should include all the variables and even introduce new ones if that will take the thing forward in your best interests. Never give anything away for nothing. If you are making a concession there must always be a condition.

At the end of the negotiation someone needs to make a closing statement or question. You will never know if you got all the concessions the other party was willing to make or if you would have had to give away more if the negotiation had continued. Start by deciding where you intend to stop conceding and then ask yourself if the time has come to summarise the solution and invite them to agree. Not too

Career case in point

One of my customers used to send me a draft contract. I would look at it and query some points. His custom was quite quickly to concede a lot of those points except where he was absolutely determined not to move. At that point he sent me another contract which I signed. It was only when we had a small problem later that I discovered his habit of changing other items in the contract as well as the ones that I had queried. I don't like such a technique since it runs the risk of making someone feel badly misled, but watch out for it.

soon so you lose credibility, but soon enough to have a conclusion that both parties feel good about. Don't forget to write down all the points that you have agreed. It is an old trick to add one or two points in the letter of agreement sent out after the meeting, so make sure you have a comprehensive note of what was agreed.

One last point on negotiating with customers. From your career point of view it is important that your customers look good to their managers, and that they see you as helping them with this. They move to other departments or to other companies, and they may well have relevance to your barnstorming progress. The unwritten fact of life here is 'You will do well, if I do well.' So, in negotiation, make sure they do not feel bad about what you have done, even if it costs a bit more of your company's money. Look at the deal from their perspective as well as your own. Try to give a minor concession or two that is unimportant to you but can help your opposite number get the whole deal approved by his boss. That way you safeguard the vital improvements you have won and will win again because the same supplier executive will be trusted with the next negotiation. In other words, lose a few tactical battles to win the war. The opportunities for doing this with internal customers are excellent, you can talk each other up and help each other climb the career ladder. I think they call that a win/win situation.

Idea 52 – Save on facilities

One of the suggestions Robert Townsend makes in his excellent book *Up the Organisation* is that the board of directors should live in accommodation that monks would find rather spartan, and make the facilities for data input operators lavish. He has a point. If you are the manager you don't need to have an office that pushes this fact down everyone's throat. It is not a question of looking like the manager – you are the manager and your behaviour will say that without the highest-backed chair, esplanade-sized office space and antique mahogany desk. Here is a place where spending frugally is just right.

This is the sort of approach that people who own their own businesses take, so why is it not good for managers running someone else's business? If it does not help your career, spend money in a way that makes Scrooge at the start of the book look profligate.

Example

I was visiting the managing director of a small but fast growing advertising agency. I walked through reception, very smart, past a conference room decorated in fashionable and expensive style through a door leading to the offices. 'Here we are', he said. 'What, you stand in the corridor?', I joked. 'No, I work in here', he said and opened the door to the cupboard under the stairs. This held a small table and a fold-up chair that allowed him to sit half in the corridor and half in the cupboard.

Idea 53 – Think big and don't look small

Once you have arrived at a certain seniority and trust, you will have considerable freedom to spend the company's money with little chance that the odd misdemeanour will be discovered. Still don't do it, because you could look small to someone – your boss, your people or even your suppliers and customers.

In one of my lecture tours around the USA I was booked by a company to talk to its staff in some 12 cities around the country. Included in these were a number on the east coast. I was therefore somewhat surprised that one of the people who worked for my main sponsor and was based in Boston announced that he was coming to see me in San Francisco. I assumed that he had to be in San Francisco about that time anyway. How wrong I was. He flew in on the overnight plane and went off to the airport to return to Boston once I had finished the day's work. Subsequently I asked him why, and he said, 'Don't tell anyone Ken, but I did it for the Frequent Flier Miles. I use them for trips to Europe with my wife.' I suppose it did not matter, but I thought poorly of this. After all, the company does actually pay for Frequent Flier Miles, and this is exactly the sort of budget that gets cut when things are tight. 'Cheapskate', I thought.

Oh, and if you do get offered first class on an aeroplane, try it out once by all means; but nowadays business class is not far behind and it's half the price.

Six Greatest Ideas for Spending the Organisation's Money Cleverly

Introduction

Have you ever tried to argue with a finance director? They don't play fair. They have at their disposal an army of jargon, calculated, correct words, to wrong-foot any up-and-coming manager. Take managers promoted into facing new challenges. They are trained for the physical task they have been assigned, but have no experience of the bunch of financial hurdles and measures that come with the job. The rising star needs to correct this imbalance and work out how to use the way finance works to their advantage. You can make money out of nothing, if you know what you are doing like *the property developers, Idea 57*, and there are many rules of thumb such as the *rule of 72 Idea 56* that will help you through the financial maelstrom, but let's start where so many managers get blind-sided, the internal accounting system.

Idea 54 – Watch out there are management accounts about

If you ignore the financial side of your job you will start to lose control of the physical task. If you get behind with the administration it's only going to get worse. If you do not query figures which appear to be wrong, particularly cross charges coming in from other parts of the business, you could find yourself carrying a huge load of costs dumped on you by someone who has learnt their way around the system, and has seen you coming. Even if there is no one in your organisation with such evil intent, you must not rely on the internal costing systems, they are very difficult to get right and are notoriously inaccurate. The difficulty is to make the systems keep up with changes in the organisation and you need to be thoroughly aware of how the systems work, or they may deny you stardom through assessing your financial performance as being below par.

Another area where financial hazards lurk is the divisional system many companies deploy. This involves cross charging and has huge traps for the unwary. Find out how your organisation does it and then look for anomalies. These frequently show up when a deal involving a series of transactions does not make sense for each individual division, though attractive to the organisation as a whole. When you spot something like that, you can either take the case to senior management, perhaps by putting a paper up, or manipulate the system to suit you. After all, if you are making an extra two per cent in this way, it means that one of your competitor managers is losing it.

Career case in point

Most internal accounting systems allocate the overheads of the organisation to departments or profit centres in some way. If they do it in the simplest possible way – based on turnover – you can actually expand your business and reduce your profits. Suppose you supply an internal telephone service to other departments in the organisation. You charge them rental for their equipment and charge them for their calls. The calls side is becoming increasingly low margin, and you may only be able to charge a very small amount, say 1%, above the rate that you pay your supplier for your supervision of the service. If, however, your management overheads are charged as 3% of turnover, then each call made will actually damage your profits, and any expansion of the service will exacerbate this effect. It may seem unlikely when put like this, but it happens all the time.

Idea 55 – Keep in with suppliers

We talked about making your customers look good in the idea about negotiating. Don't forget that the 'If I do well, you do well' unwritten rule operates here too. Your suppliers are a brilliant source of market information, including any relevant competitive data, and should be cherished. The last point to check before you do a deal is 'What are the consequences of this deal on my career?' Spend cleverly to please and impress your suppliers as well as your managers.

Idea 56 – Rule of 72

This is a very useful rule of compound interest. Unfortunately it is not a mathematical formula so it does not work with very short timescales. But for timescales of longer than 2 years it works well enough. To calculate how long it will take for money to double at a given rate of compound interest, simply divide 72 by the interest rate. Thus at an interest rate of 10%, money will double in just over seven years. And you can use it the other way round. If I want to double my money in five years what compound annual interest rate will I require? 72 divided by 5 gives you a rate of round about 14.5%.

You will probably not use it so often, but as a matter of interest, so to speak, tripling your money works in the same way with the rule of 115.

Idea 57 – Imitate the property developer

How do you make money from property without having anything to do with the physical purchase or management of it? The answer is – become a property developer. The value of a property lies in its ability to generate income through rents. There are three elements that make up this ability: the capital to buy the land and pay for the property to be built, the expertise to build the property, and a tenant and system for paying the rent. A property developer, interestingly enough, has none of these attributes. What they have is knowledge. They know investors with money looking for a property opportunity, they are forewarned when land and properties are coming on the market, they know builders who are looking for work and they keep close contacts with estate agents and others in the business of finding tenants and administering tenancies. Put this together and you have a property deal, with the developer taking his or her percentage from all the people who actually do the work.

Look for such opportunities yourself. Not only outside your organisation but also inside it. Check how you can put to good use what you know without any increase in your budget or the taking on of new skills. Don't forget the databases you have built up over the years or your customers. Could anyone make money out of the former or sell something else to the latter? After all you don't need anything to get into property – apart from knowledge.

Idea 58 – Entertain wisely as well as well

Whether it is for your staff, or internal colleagues or customers and suppliers, the entertainment budget is a powerful weapon for getting things done your way. Focus it. There is no point in taking a person with no interest in opera to Covent Garden, nor, of course their spouse. It is a travesty of entertainment if people go away muttering about pretentiousness and being bored. Know your quarry. Find out what they do like and lay that on.

If you have the money then entertain in style. Lunch at the Ritz but with only the menu of the day, is probably not as good as freedom of choice in a slightly less upmarket restaurant. Style means doing things properly and making the entertainment time memorable. You can do this even on a small budget. If lunch has to be a working one, get something more interesting than cheese sandwiches. Find a deli that offers a wide choice or do it yourself.

Idea 59 – Be civilised but flexibly

The wider you are read and cultured the better. Width includes being comfortable to eat at the Ritz and enjoying stopping at the local greasy spoon for a bacon sandwich with brown sauce. You must never pretend to know something that you don't, but make an effort. If you do have to go to the opera, read something about it and perhaps listen to it a couple of times so that it becomes a little familiar. Just showing interest is enough, you are not expected to become an expert.

Culturally too, it is worth thinking about your local environment. I am a Scot, and when the English came north we were ever so grateful if they had taken the trouble to know that the concert hall in Edinburgh is the Usher Hall and that Raith Rovers play at Kirkcaldy. It was nice when they did not think that SNO (the Scottish National Orchestra) is part of a brewery or that the Edinburgh Fringe was a hairstyle. They did not need to become Scotophiles, just have enough interest to know that Burns is not treated at the Western General.

Idea 60 – The greatest idea for becoming top dog now

Let's take a break for the moment because I have just realised that if you have read this far, you now know enough to short cut the whole career business, become a senior manager and build a retirement fund in two years. There is a catch. You need some capital. I will later illustrate the idea assuming you have £50,000, which is feasible for those with equity in their homes, whilst acknowledging that it will take more than two years starting from there. But first look at this end game, which involves having £1 million to start with.

First set your objective using *pinpoint the destination Idea 10*, to make sure it is a SMART objective:

The objective is to be the chief executive officer of a company earning profits of £20 million, own 25% of the shares in the company and have £5 million in the bank within two years. Yes, that looks smart enough.

Using financial leverage *Idea 16*, arrange a facility to borrow £9 million on condition that you can find a suitable company to buy for your £1 million and the bank's £9 million.

Using good negotiation technique *Idea 51*, buy for the price of £10 million a company that made profits last year of £1 million. This, from how you value a company *Idea 39*, puts it on a modest multiple or price/earnings ratio of 10.

Using *the rule of 72 Idea 56*, realise that to double your profits in two years you need a growth rate of 36% per annum. Actually because this is such a short timescale the rule of 72 is slightly inaccurate, so let's aim for 40%.

Using *the rule of 2% Idea 50*, increase next year's profits by 46%. This puts you a bit ahead of the game and next year you only need to improve by 35%. So using

Ideas 40 and *41*, create and implement a strategy that will achieve this. Your strategy will indicate where you have to make changes in how your people have to go about their jobs; so make these changes using *rule of 20% Idea 44*. Your profits at the end of year two are £2 million. Well done.

Using your presentation skills *Idea 27*, float the company on the stock exchange using the same modest price earnings multiple of 10. This values the company at £20 million. Now sell £15 million worth of shares and pay off the bank; with costs and interest this will take about £10 million. Bank the other £5 million and congratulate yourself, modestly, on achieving your objective. You are top dog and rich. You have £5 million in the bank and £5 million worth of shares. Now make it an Internet company, and multiply everything by a hundred!

If you only have £50,000, it will take 3 iterations of the cycle. After the first cycle you will have £500,000 and after the second £5 million. You could, of course, stop there.

But if you, like me, cannot make this sudden leap, read on and do it the harder way.

Six Greatest Ideas for Spending the Organisation's Money Lavishly

Introduction

Spending frugally is good advice when you are trying to impress people with your financial performance and sagacity, but it is the opposite of what suits your career in some circumstances. No matter what strictures management bandy about suggesting that 'good managers are the ones who spend the company's money as though it were their own', the truth is that it is not their own and it hurts them naught to chuck it around when the time is right. Use it fundamentally to get people who may be important to you on your side. You may want to join a consultancy at some point so cultivate them for a start *Idea 64*, and don't be shy in spending on the creature comforts of the top brass *Idea 65*.

Idea 61 – Hunt the headhunter

Later in this book, the director of human resources of Vodafone Airtouch is going to suggest that you need to change jobs and organisations every two years; so spend lavishly on headhunters. These people are very expensive so it is not difficult. But they have an encyclopaedic knowledge of your industry and the people and opportunities in it. They have to have; and they are very brazen about contacting people and keeping it that way. Encourage them to make suggestions to you at any time, not just when you want people. That way you are also encouraging them to do the same in terms of job opportunities for you.

Be very careful of the current fad for 'head-shunting'. This involves getting a headhunter to place a person you are trying to get rid of into another company. By

Career clue
from the
Boardroom

*Be polite to
people as you
move up - you
will probably
meet them on
your way down.*

Gordon M.W.
Owen CBE
(Chairman,
Energis)

doing it this way you avoid the expense of severance pay, and remove any threat of being sued for wrongful dismissal. But, it would seem that some-one who discovers that the ploy has been visited on them can still sue for unfair dismissal, and if the receiving company believes it has been duped, it also might have a case.

Idea 62 – Fire at will – gracefully

We have already remarked how small a world the upper reaches of any industry are. You come across people whom you served as a customer or for whom you worked, frequently enough to make sure that you only make enemies when there is no alternative. You may also come across people who worked for you in an earlier life, which means, of course, that you may come across people whom you fired. Sacking people is not a job that most managers find pleasant; so here are the *dos* and *don'ts* of it:

- Do prepare carefully, not only for the meeting but also for what will happen in personnel terms after it.
- Don't let the firee talk you out of it. If you have decided, do it. You will never recover with this person if you change your mind.
- Do have a stiff brandy before the meeting. You need to look assertive, firm and friendly, not a nervous wreck. Remember the other person is the one with the problem.
- Don't relax too much, they will probably not find jokes amusing at this time.
- Do give a generous if not lavish settlement. This sugars the pill greatly and if you go beyond the company's norms, the person you are firing will know that it is you being generous, not the rules.
- Do go through the process meticulously. It is important that it is you who gives the generous settlement not an industrial tribunal.

- Don't let the human-resources rules delay something that needs to be done. Buy your way out of it if necessary.

Career clue from the boardroom

Idea 63 – Use the best brains

Saint Vincent de Paul said 'If, in order to succeed in an enterprise I were obliged to choose between fifty deer commanded by a lion and fifty lions commanded by a deer, I should consider myself more certain of success with the first group than the second.' Mmm, up to a point, St Vincent; but what about fifty lions led by a lion, much more likely to succeed. There is always contention amongst the upwardly mobile about whether first-class brains in your team are an opportunity or a threat. I am convinced that using the best people gets the best career results. So they want your job; they will actually have to perform then, as well as try politically to look as though they, not you, are the inspiration behind the team's success.

A young person in any organisation should know the limit of his or her authority, when to exceed it, and to make sure that he is right.

A chairman

Get good people under you both as staff and as consultants, and pay them lavishly. A contented consultant has a boss who talks to your boss's boss's boss and has good credibility when he or she mentions how well you are doing. Well-paid staff are more likely to stay, and, of course, no one expects you to earn less than them. The other thing about the best brains is that they are in your indus-

---

Career clue

Choose a business which has an output you find enjoyable and interesting, always employ outstanding people beneath you, treat everyone with respect and accept that change is an opportunity not a threat.

Chairman, FTSE 100 company

try and you never know when you might meet them again. Not in the short-term maybe, but even ten years later people remember those who did them some good.

Idea 64 – Choose and work with the right consultants

The *Economist* in an article in February 1998 said a lot. Entitled 'Management Consultancy; the new witch doctors' it started 'If you had to pick a single business or profession that typifies the frenetic second half of the 20th century, it might well be management consultancy. It has grown fast … it is easy to get into … it pays well … and, best of all, nobody can agree precisely what it is.'

In choosing a consultant it is first necessary to assign priorities to the skills and qualities needed.

Ask yourself:

- What is the purpose in hiring a consultant?
- What can an outside agency do that internal staff cannot?

Once you have selected a consultant, several safeguards must be put in place. These safeguards will ensure the smooth running of the relationship with the consultant and will mean the most effective use of their time as possible:

- *Have a formal contract*
- *Payment*
  You need an agreement of schedule of payment and what constitutes chargeable expenses.
- *The decision makers*
  Establish who is to do what. How much authority will the consultancy firm have? Also, lines of communication need to be made clear for any problems or queries that may arise.

- *Cancellation or postponement fee*
  This must be reflected in a formal contract.

Why use a management consultant?

- *Staffing issues*
  It may simply be a matter of time and money. That is, that you do not have the appropriate staffing levels to undertake the work needed and it may be impracticable to employ more for what may be a short-term need. Or it may be that, after doing some number crunching, it appears that it is more cost effective to use a consultancy firm than to do the work internally.
- *Speciality*
  The issue a particular organisation faces might be best resolved by seeking the advice of people with a particular speciality. This enables you to use this speciality for the problem in hand but also to learn from the consultancy firm for the future. Sometimes an organisation gets into a situation where 'it cannot see the wood for the trees'. An outsider may be able to cast a new light on matters.
- *Politics*
  We have seen that one of the major issues that you have to deal with is company politics, the messy stuff that gets in the way of getting a job done. It is inevitable once you add the unpredictable element of people into any situation. An outside consultancy firm may be able to provide an unbiased view to a third party and provide a more accepted opinion (although it will often be the same opinion) than you. And then there is always the added bonus that external advisers can take the blame for unpopular but necessary solutions to problems; thus preserving your reputation.

Career clue
from the
boardroom

*If you know that
you are per-
forming well do
not be afraid to
ask for promo-
tion or greater
responsibility.*

George Paul
(Chairman,
Norwich Union)

Consultancy itself could be a smart move for you. Their partners are extremely well paid. So bear that in mind as you work with them, and for goodness sake spend your company's money lavishly – everybody needs a friend.

Idea 65 – Look after top management

If you have not met a senior manager with whom you are about to come into contact, you will, of course, prepare yourself by talking to people who have. But there are one or two assumptions that you might have to make. One of these is vanity. All human beings are to some extent vain. Top managers are somewhat larger than life human beings therefore senior managers tend to have as high a level of vanity as any normal human being and higher than most.

Example

A manager in the Edinburgh office of a US company was about to get a historic visit from the chief executive who was visiting the UK. The manager, we will call him Tom, knew that his counterpart in the Manchester office, we'll call him Mike, had his visit a few days earlier. The plan in each case was that the CEO would fly up from London and spend two days visiting the offices and meeting customers. There would be a customer dinner on the evening of the first day. Tom asked Mike about his preparations. 'Well,' said Mike, 'it's difficult. You know that we are being asked to save on expenses at the moment so I thought that we should show that we take that seriously and keep the whole visit fairly low key.' 'Really?' said Tom. 'Yes,' continued Mike, 'I thought we would pick him up in a normal first-line manager's company car, that would show thrift, and we are going to put him up in the same hotel we use for the graduate trainees when they join. It is pleasant but obviously not overly expensive.' He continued to describe this hair-shirt treatment. At the end of the conversation Tom called in his PA and said 'We are going to give the man a welcome to Edinburgh that makes the plans for the Queen coming up to Holyrood Palace look stingy.'

And so they did. After his visit to Manchester the CEO was not entirely looking forward to the next one. He arrived at the airport to be met by a PA with a clipboard, and was led straight past the luggage carousel to a waiting large limousine complete with peaked cap driver. The PA explained that someone else was picking up his bags. This happened and his bags were taken to the sort of Georgian Hotel that even a well-travelled executive finds unusual. A butler unpacked them and put his things away.

Tom had booked a suite so that the CEO could entertain the top few customers in Scotland privately with drinks before they descended to join the *hoi polloi* customers for dinner. And so it went on.

Subsequently Tom got feedback that the CEO had loved the visit to Edinburgh. In fact he got a warm thank-you note, while Mike just got a note, and another one from his boss saying 'Do not do that again.'

Take Tom's advice. When it comes to senior managers spend lavishly and never ever underestimate anyone's vanity.

Idea 66 – Advertise yourself

If you are responsible for some or all of the advertising budget, negotiate it up as high as you can. An effective advertising campaign can make you famous not only within the company but externally as well; so spend, spend, spend.

Eight Greatest Ideas for Things to Do Differently If You Are a Woman

Introduction

I have spoken with a number of women in writing this and, although it seems good advice to me, I by definition have no direct experience of what is being said. I am much more the editor of this section rather than the author. The clue seems to be to avoid your gender being an issue, which is why deliberately avoiding behaviour that men consistently associate negatively with women, is probably right *Idea 68*. It was best summarised by one woman who explained a point and then said, 'In that case people will simply not notice that you are a woman in a man's world, which is what you are looking for.' That having been said, it appears that women should use their gender-oriented talents to the full *Idea 71*. The first idea is about simple and obnoxious prejudice.

Idea 67 – Lie your head off

There was a *Panorama* programme earlier this year that carried this message: if you are a woman in your late 20s or 30s, you are likely to be discriminated against if you go for a promotion or for a new job. The reason it gave is that managers are prejudiced against such women because, if they have children, they may have to take some time off to look after them; or, if they do not have children, they may take maternity leave in order to start a family. The discriminators are found to be not only men, but also women who are themselves opting not to have children in their 30s.

If this is true – and who am I to question *Panorama*? – this is surely an occasion for women to ignore the strictures of Robert Townsend never to con anyone, or this book's advice not to lie on your CV. Lie your head off. Leave the kids out of the equation. Perhaps you might hint at the fact that it just isn't to be, and that in the circumstances you are going to channel your energies into a career rather than a family. This is probably not very good, but you will be able to improve on it.

Perhaps the only way to attack this problem is for the government to legislate for paternity leave to be the same length of time as maternity leave, and for it to be compulsory within a certain timescale. Then, perhaps, give men and women equal rights for extra time off when their kids are young. Somehow get the whole population to play on a level playing field.

Women have given me some other suggestions for what to do apart from lying your head off:

- Put off becoming a parent until your 40s (you can always freeze your eggs).
- Have children and get your partner to stay at home while you go out to work.

There are some people who defend the current situation, saying that maternity leave and taking time off for the kids discriminates against shareholders by damaging the profits of the organisation. This can't be true, can it? For a start it seems more damaging to the shareholders to ignore the talents of half the managers in that age group. (Frankly, I know some male managers whose general incompetence would probably kill a baby left in their charge, so goodness knows what they will do to their bits of their businesses.) And in the end most shareholders are people building pension funds or pensioners. If there are more men building pension funds than women, then this is a result of this discrimination, and there are certainly more women pensioners than men. Pensioners live off equities; therefore giving equal rights to women managers cannot damage the interests of shareholders. QED.

Idea 68 – Try not to conform to their stereotype

Some men will call the same behaviour in a man and a woman as 'authoritative and assertive' in the first case and 'bossy' in the second. Perhaps you need to seed more 'please's and 'thank-you's into your instructions as a result of this. Look for a consensual way of giving instructions, unless of course you run the danger of being less effective. Or is this pandering to men's prejudices? Gosh, it's complicated. But senior women have said to me that as long as this is the current situation you have to work with it. Similarly don't be too often, or at the wrong time, seen to be gossiping. Men and women all do it, but again it has a negative stereotype with some men if women are plainly indulging themselves amongst themselves.

Most men dress smartly in the morning and then pay no further attention to their appearance for the rest of the day. People notice if women spend a lot of time during the day using mirrors and repairing themselves. The advice I am given is to imitate men on this one. Look professional and then forget about it.

Idea 69 – Don't get a thing about it

It does not matter who opens the door for whom. If you are dealing with a man who insists on opening the door for you, it does not make much sense to glare at him as if he were being condescending. Equally, do not expect men to open the door for you. This goes for all the other mores that my parents' generation thought constituted manners. You want to stand out in the crowd for your talents and skills, and as such to make your gender irrelevant.

Idea 70 – Don't get tarred with the PA brush

Good advice to women some years ago was much more simple in this regard – do not learn to type. Such advice is as silly to give now as to suggest that a woman should not learn to read.

Now I know that everyone does their own typing nowadays, but most people, particularly in the early part of their career, will do work that looks secretarial or belongs to a personal assistant. Indeed it can be a smart move for either gender to get close to the corridors of power by helping senior managers out with their letter and report writing and filing. Women have to do it in such a way that it is clear that this is not their career. One of the worst things a male colleague can say about you is that you are efficient, that you collect good information for decision making but that you are no decision maker.

Idea 71 – Act like a woman, not like a man

Women might think that they have to be tough, ruthless and masculine to scale the dizzying heights of the career ladder, but in fact the reverse seems to be true. Research suggests that women, being generally more efficient and trustworthy, generous with praise, and with a better understanding of their workforce, make better managers than men.

A survey published at the end of last year by *Management Today* magazine revealed that the majority of those questioned – 1000 male and female managers across the UK – believed that women had a more modern outlook on their profession and were more open-minded and considerate. A similar number, by contrast, believed that male managers were egocentric and more likely to steal the credit for work done by others. (See this book *passim*.)

A survey of female bosses in the US also supports this theory. A five-year study of 2500 managers from 450 firms found that staff of both sexes rated many male bosses to be self-obsessed and autocratic. Women on the other hand, were found to be the front-runners when building teamwork and communicating with staff.

So make sure you show that caring, considerate, nurturing side – it will win you friends among the ranks as well as in higher places – and everyone will be delighted when you move on up a rung.

Idea 72 – Choose a male-dominated profession

You might have to work hard to overcome prejudices at first, but you could win big time in the long term. With equal rights very firmly on the media agenda and very much at the forefront of public consciousness, a lot of men nowadays must be seen to be even-handed when it comes to recruiting or promoting the female gender. If they discriminate against women, they could be in big trouble. If you join a profession where women at the top are still rare, the men will be so scared that you're going to run off screaming 'discrimination' that they'll positively do what they can to avoid it. Also, remember that if there aren't many women around, who's going to be that one female representative on the board? Get in there quick – it could be you.

Idea 73 – Get them used to e-mail

Some women regard e-mail as a mighty useful aid to handling absence due to kids. If everyone is very used to your communicating frequently in this way, they will not know if you are writing your e-mails in the office or while you are doing the 2.00 a.m. feed.

Idea 74 – Flirt your head off

I have included all the advice I got from the women I spoke to, so I will pass on this piece from a senior executive in the insurance industry. She said that, in the early years of her career especially, she flirted outrageously with her customers on the telephone. When asked if she continued to do this when face-to-face she said 'No' rather sternly. Other women reacted to the flirting technique with surprise and, I have to say, total disagreement.

Four Greatest Ways for Managing Projects

Introduction

You build a successful career on going the extra mile. As well as carrying out your function to plan, there are many other opportunities to get involved with projects of a one-off nature.

This means managing projects, and everyone needs to be able to prepare a project plan *Idea 76*, and assume the necessary style of leadership of the team *Idea 77*. But let's start by making sure that you recognise a project when it comes along.

Career clue from the boardroom

For those individuals who are motivated and aspire to the most senior leadership roles, my advice would be to undertake many different, broad-ranging and stretching assignments. The key is to learn as much about the business environment as possible, and develop an insight into the different disciplines which leaders need to understand to be successful. These include leading people, managing performance, marketing, operations, finance and technology. The world of business is becoming increasingly more challenging. Successful leaders will be those who retain clarity and focus in this demanding and ever more complex environment.

Chris Wathen (Director, Group Human Resources, NatWest Group)

Idea 75 – Nothing can go wrong because nothing is planned

In days gone by, project management was the business of engineers who used the techniques of project management to control complex activities. Nowadays, it is wise for all managers to make themselves aware of how to take a list of activities and treat it as a project. The stovepipe image of separate functions operating on their own is giving way to cross-functional teams, and they need to be managed. Projects are good too if you want to operate in high profile.

There is a fair amount of work to do up-front in managing a project and, generally speaking, managers fail to go to the initial trouble of creating a project when they should. They try to manage a series of activities and come a cropper. The rule of thumb for realising that you need to announce a project has three elements:

- The timescale from start to finish is more than a month, often a lot longer.
- There is more than one function involved.
- You do not have direct authority over all the people resources needed.

If these three elements are in place, go to your boss and propose that they become the sponsor of the project. Outline your vision for how things will look once the project is complete. Make sure the timing is right. If there are a lot of initiatives

---

Career clue

Look at something difficult that needs to be done; for example, some major change that the organisation needs to make. Perhaps your boss has not thought of it or has thought it too tough, but he or she would be happy to take the credit for it. Offer to manage it, and deliver.

Career clue

A good result is much more impressive if you have previously signalled it in a plan. (You may wish to reveal the plan after the result has occurred, of course.) Never let it be said of you 'All your plans are unsuccessful and all your successes are unplanned'.

---

already started, you may run the danger of starting something you cannot finish. If your vision is bold and useful enough, you may even cause your boss to cancel someone else's pet project to divert resource to your new one. In this case make sure you are the first person to sympathise with the thwarted colleague, 'But what could I do, you know what he's like when he has the bit between his teeth?'

The key to this period in the plan is assessing the chances of success. Use the project-management technique of driving and restraining forces to predict the chances of the project succeeding. Driving forces are strong if they include closing a competitive gap, or gaining competitive edge. They are strong if they translate easily into sales growth and so on. Restraining forces are the natural resistance that people have to change and current workload. Remember, most projects aimed at improving the working environment generate activities in addition to people's normal jobs. Now produce a forcefield analysis by comparing the impact of the driving and restraining forces. A bar chart will do with the x-axis calibrated from +10 for the driving forces, to −10 for the restraining. The y-axis has the list of forces. This produces a very good diagrammatic clue as to the chances of success and a neat presentation aid when you go to your sponsor for backing.

Finally, think about roughly how much resource you will need and how available it is likely to be. Try to negotiate for this outline resource plan now, before you have volunteered to take on the task. Make a list of all the stakeholders, people who will in some way be impacted by the project. These will include the key team members as well as your customers and possibly your suppliers. At some point you have to get them all on board, so make sure the list is complete. Think about how much authority your sponsor has, and wriggle out of any project where the sponsor is totally incompetent at getting his or her own way, or hated sufficiently for people to want anything they touch to fail.

Idea 76 – Making a plan

Now you need a plan. Fatten out the vision statement by getting the key stakeholders to add their views. If it is difficult to predict exactly how things will be after the project, try taking a blank sheet of paper and writing down the ideal. It may be unattainable, so be careful how you show this bit to customers, but it gives an aiming point that the team can take into account as they produce the purpose and objectives of the project. The purpose is a one-liner showing what you are going to do, by when, and what is the cost constraint. For example, 'We are going to produce a new system for communicating with our customers. It will be in place before the end of this company year and will cost no more than £50,000 to do.'

The objectives of the project are the business aims of the team. If the team achieves its purpose, what will be the impact on sales, costs, profits, cashflow and

---

Career clue

Do not forget why you are doing this project. It is to widen your knowledge of the business and impress your seniors. If you have achieved this at as early a stage as this, it may very well be time to pass it on to someone else. You do not want to get bogged down and find it difficult to take up a new opportunity, just because the project is not finished.

customer satisfaction? For each objective, formulate an indicator showing where you are now, and where you intend to be after the project. Be realistic, but if the sponsor is going to spend money or ask their boss for it, these objectives must be worthwhile. Normally there are one or two improvements you can allocate to your project that are going to happen even if the project team went on a bicycling tour of the highlands. Do so.

List the constraints now. Set the boundaries of what you are not going to do as accurately as you set them for what you are going to do. Disappointment is a careerist's nightmare so avoid it by making sure that no-one thinks that your project includes the impossible or the undesirable from your point of view.

You are ready for the plan now. Get the stakeholders to brainstorm the list of activities necessary to complete the project. Don't worry about order at this stage, just make sure you have a comprehensive list. Include in the list some start-up activities – remember, you're doing this high-profile – communication activities where you tell everyone who needs to know what you are doing, and close-down activities that will involve your boss in claiming the kudos of a difficult job well done and you in taking a modest degree of credit for making it happen. Banging your drum is best done in private, and there will be time enough for you to explain to your boss's boss that it was all your idea and, believe it or not, you have got another one.

Career clue from the boardroom

At one time, people were expected to simply get on with their job and not worry about the 'whole' picture. These days people have to understand the whole of the business to ensure that they can work in a cross-matrix way and are able to move swiftly across the business to areas of greatest need.

John A. Hart (Group Personnel Director, PowerGen)

The activities should now fall quite easily into groups and reveal the phases of the project. You will mark each phase with some form of PR campaign. Remember that as your project goes along, other people will be having ideas for new ones. To protect the resources allocated to your project, you have to keep showing progress along the way. The marketing people call these activities 'mid-life kickers' and you should plan for them at this stage. Don't forget how *you* got the resources.

Career clue

It is often possible for you to make your boss's boss look like a star. This is always good news, so seek it out.

Now put the activities and groups of activities into the order in which the team will complete them. Use a network diagram and critical path analysis to find where there could be problems in delivering on time. If you do not understand critical path analysis, learn about it; it's quite easy and rather fun. Alternatively get someone who is a whiz on project network software to take on the task of project co-ordinator.

Once you have the activities and their order, you are in a position to produce the resource requirement. Don't just concentrate on people. You will also require information gathering and access, facilities, equipment and materials. Try to be as complete as you can. Soon this stuff is going to be in front of a finance person, and if there is one thing such people love, it is discovering a missing cost in the list of resources. This reduces the credibility of the whole proposition and gives them the enormous satisfaction of kicking it into touch. As a general rule I have found that if you make a finance person's day, you have probably done yourself some harm.

A word on costing projects. You can, of course, simply work out the cost for every resource the project is going to use. This is quite easy but leads to some anomalies. You may, for example be paying for a person who is only working on your project part time, and paying, as it were, for the elapsed time of activities rather than man-hours. You may be paying for a computer that would be doing nothing if it were not for your project. Such costs are known as sunk costs and should not be attributed to your project. The whole process is known as marginal costing and, if you don't understand it, get a book on it.

Career clue

Use educators and mentors, and never turn down any training course, no matter how stupid or irrelevant it seems at the time. It may come in useful some time, it goes on your CV and it is an excellent use of other people's money.

From the indicators you calculated at objectives time and these costs, you can build your cost benefit analysis. Taking this seriously is unusual, therefore you should go about it with meticulous pedantry. When you are spending company money, it is dangerous not to be able to show what the company is getting out of it. You can look extravagant and the cash plug can be pulled if times get hard.

Finally, check your plan. Speak to anyone who has got relevant experience inside or outside your organisation. Go through it, and convince yourself that if you carry out these activities, you will get that result. Use a devil's advocate to try to convince you that it is going to be a disaster. If they do convince you, don't go ahead. You can still get brownie points by showing the powers that be that you have finally proved that this is not a good path to go down. Well done.

Idea 77 – Mix up styles of leadership

There are arguments that say leaders are born and cannot be created by training and experience. It is true that your ability to get on with people is, at least to some extent, your starting point for being a leader. But you can look at some techniques in leadership and develop your natural ability to make things happen, whatever your basic talent. Think first about motivation. Leadership is the skill of persuading people to co-operate willingly to achieve results. The *willingly* is key; you cannot force motivation on people; they have to want to do a good job. It is interesting that Dale

Carnegie Training has as one of its guiding principles of leadership 'Nobody is more persuasive than a good listener.' You have to listen and observe the people in your team to decide what is the best way to motivate each of them individually. It's not rocket science; it just involves getting to know them and their needs and wants.

You will also find that good team players tend to become good team leaders. I think this is because they understand the fundamentals of team membership despite their ability to think somewhat selfishly at the same time about their careers. Team membership is much to do with trust and respect, so do not let fellow members down. If, in the worst case, you believe that a weak link in the team is going to threaten the success of the team, try to make them expose the problem themselves rather than blowing the whistle.

Leadership of a project team is on a continuum from simple directives to group discussion and consensus. You will find yourself at both ends of this continuum and at many places in the middle. As a non-executive director put it, 'You can play your

---

Career case in point

Mike Brierley, sometime captain of the England cricket team, was reckoned by an Australian fast bowler to have 'a degree in people'. Bob Willis, a fast bowler in Brierley's side, told the story that he was involved in Brierley's short-term winding up of the buccaneer cricketer Ian Botham. When he felt that Botham needed to be gingered up, he would signal to Willis who went up to Botham and told him that Mike had told him to say that Botham was bowling like a girl. Pity the poor batsman who faced the next ball from a seething Botham.

Interestingly Willis concluded the story by saying that if the captain had used the same words with him it would have destroyed his confidence and had the opposite effect. Useful things, degrees in people.

role hands-off if it works, but the opposite of hands-off management is scruff-of-the-neck.'

Whatever your style, do not lose your focus. Good leaders always aim at the objective and have their eyes on the big picture. This allows them, from time to time, to lose a battle but win the war. They are quick to admit their own mistakes and weaknesses and demonstrate their reliance on other members of the team. It is usually bad leadership technique to exude the fact that you could do all the jobs of team members better than they. Good leaders are slow to criticise and 99 times out of 100 will do it constructively. They will be destructive only when that is the best way of motivating the person being criticised.

Career clue

People work for money but do a bit extra for recognition, praise and reward.

Morale in a team goes up and down. The key here is to detect a lowering of morale, and to do something about it before it blows up into a crisis such as someone leaving or a resistance to accepting change. Low and high morale comes from personal feelings and problems outside the work place as well as from job-related issues. You will help to build morale by giving everyone an opportunity to contribute useful ideas. (Oh no, we are back to listening.) You will lower morale if a team member does not understand the relationship between what they are doing and the total picture.

So, show a genuine interest in other people, communicate well and be very objective-oriented and you will probably become a born leader.

Idea 78 – Take smart risks

The opposite of delivering on time and within budget is to disappoint. Yet all successful career people emphasise the need to take risks. In business, high return reflects high risk, and that goes for your career too. You must all the time assess the risk of any project you have volunteered for, but there are some techniques that might help towards the end of the planning phase. Remember, you are assessing the risk of the project to the business, but also the more important risk – to your career.

The business benefits of a successful project fall into three categories. They are reductions in cost, avoidance of costs, and benefits – often improvements in sales – that occur because you have changed how you do business in a way that improves your control and decision-making. Let us suppose that you are preparing a cost benefit analysis that the finance people will look at. Categorising the benefits in this way kills two birds with one stone. It will help you to understand the possibility of disappointment, and it will strengthen your hand with finance.

Reduction in costs

In any assessment of a spending project, this area is likely to be very important. Finance people are likely to agree that a reduction of costs is the most tangible benefit there is. If you are replacing one thing with another there is a good chance that the cost will be saved. Make sure that the costs claimed as a reduction are relevant, or the finance folk will bounce them. Relevant cost reductions are ones that the organisation can realise. If your project will save office space, for example, this is only a relevant cost if the organisation stops paying for the space or re-allocates it to other people. If it is going to stand empty and still be paid for, it is not a relevant cost.

Avoidance of future costs

The avoidance of future costs is a slightly different concept from a straightforward reduction in costs. This brings into the business case for a project, costs which would be incurred if the project were not undertaken. It may be possible to argue that expenditure on advertising to get sales up might save the costs involved in letting people go if sales stay the same. Once again, make sure that the cost avoided is real. Avoidance of costs has intrinsically a higher risk of not materialising than the reduction of costs. The finance people believe that and it is, in any case, true.

Improvements in control

Companies are continually re-engineering their business processes. If they change their strategy in any way or react to changes in technology, they will almost certainly have to review some of their business processes. This almost always ends up with capital and revenue expenditure, and is often justified by the fact that it affords management better control over the business. This may be good enough for the people running the business, but it is not sufficiently concrete for the finance department. They want to know how this benefit will turn into cash. Suppose your business case is for an improvement to the inventory control system. Part of your benefits argument will be that, if you have better control over inventory, you will have less stock outs and therefore higher sales. Such improvements in control can be difficult to quantify but, if you do not, the finance people will not let you put them in the business case. Often these benefits will offer the biggest numbers in the benefits section, but they are intrinsically less likely to be realised than the reduction or avoidance of costs.

We have said that no estimate for the future will be exact; there will always be the unexpected as well as the normal tolerance to be expected in a prediction. Risks to the benefits are that you will deliver less than your prediction, or that you will not deliver them in time.

Here is an example of a risk matrix using the benefit type as the grouping. As well as the most likely estimate, calculate the worst scenario and an optimistic one.

	Pessimistic	Most likely	Optimistic
Reduce costs	Likelihood 1	Likelihood 3	Likelihood 6
Avoid costs	Likelihood 2	Likelihood 5	Likelihood 8
Increase revenues or control	Likelihood 4	Likelihood 7	Likelihood 9

Experience allows us to give each cell in the matrix a number from 1 to 9 in the order of confidence that we should have that the benefit will be achieved. It goes from the most likely to occur, the pessimistic estimate for a cost reduction, to the least likely, an optimistic estimate for a benefit in increased sales or improvement in control.

Assuming we know the costs involved in the project, we can now calculate whether this is a high- or low-risk project. Add up all the benefits from the cells marked 1–3. If that produces a number which is greater than the costs, the project can be termed low risk. If you have to go down to 8 or 9 before the costs are covered, you have a project that carries a high risk that the project will not deliver the benefits profitably. Think about wriggling out of it if you need the cell numbered 6. At that point the risks are rather high.

Don't forget that the objective of risk analysis is not only to identify what the risks are, but also to do something about them. If, for example, there was some doubt about the benefits in cell 5, and that doubt was the difference between a medium and high risk project, you might be inclined to do some more investigation to improve the estimate, or resolve to put extra resources into making sure that during the implementation of the project the benefits in that cell are actually realised.

In comparison with benefits, costs are more straightforward to estimate. You will find they fall into the categories of staff, equipment rental, depreciation of purchased assets, facilities and consumables. It is always better to agree costs with a supplier, since this removes any risk that they might be wrong. Once again make sure that the costs are relevant.

Risks to the costs are that they will be greater than budget, either because your estimate is wrong, or because delay has cost money. You can add contingency money to the costs at this stage and see where in the risk matrix the necessary return is achieved.

Cost benefit analysis is a closed book to the unambitious. It is therefore an opportunity for the careerist to show that he or she is willing and able to test their ideas for the way forward against a logical benchmark. Add to it the career-protecting risk assessment and you have two management techniques to make your sojourn as a project manager, or a line manager with an idea, brilliantly successful.

Six Greatest Ideas for Getting Nearer the Top

Introduction

This section could be subtitled *Back to Basics*. As you become more senior, you will find your own management style and find that it works. At this stage there is a danger that you might let your use of personality and charisma drop back in terms of your communications skills and career plan. No matter how high you have risen, you still need to avoid the pitfalls of jargon *Idea 80*, and get the right mix of heart and head when making decisions *Idea 83*. Remember that as you rise, people will give you less and less feedback on your own performance. They are less likely to challenge you if they find your communication difficult to understand; so have a look at how you write to people.

Idea 79 – Write to be understood

You cannot put it much better than the career case in point below.

Career case in point

Writing, when properly managed (as you may be sure I think mine is) is but a different name for conversation.

Laurence Sterne (author of *Tristram Shandy*)

If you want to recap on the structure of a piece of persuasive communication, it is in *present yourself well Idea 27* and *put up a paper Idea 48*. The style you want is Sterne's. The *Plain English Campaign* has been pretty successful and their annual awards for writing gobbledegook are moving inexorably towards the last bastion of formalised, difficult-to-understand English – the legal and commercial departments. Have a look at the contracts you are offering your customers. Are they still in the 'heretofore' and 'aforesaid' mode? Even insurance companies are getting there, writing paragraphs that start 'We will repair your car if …'. *I* and *We* are, thank goodness, at last being used. 'Please find enclosed …' is changing to 'I enclose …' Just keep it simple, stupid.

Idea 80 – Don't get involved in management speak

Try this little experiment. When you are sitting with a team of managers, talk gibberish for a while. Use good *Harvard Business Review* words and lots of jargon, but don't let it make sense.

> *Well, a new paradigm will help strategically but unfortunately not culturally. Fundamentally I think that is what empowerment means, particularly given the high values the company wants us to take to the market place. You boot up the new paradigm, round up the counter-enthusiasts and get every one sensible to recast their strategy. This gives you change, you see, and huge improvements in the whole dynamics of the organisation.*

Actually as I re-read that, it is probably true. It is certainly as sensible as some stuff I have heard in the training room. It is interesting that you will probably not be challenged, partly because your audience only listened to the first few words, and partly because it just could possibly make sense and they are not going to admit to not understanding it.

Top people always talk in terms others will understand, and avoid the 'flavour of the month' business babble.

Career clue from the boardroom

Idea 81 – Work towards values – but pragmatically

In order to be successful, it is important to have an understanding of what your organisation wants, or needs from you, and how what you offer meets that need.

There is a type of politician, and indeed political commentator, who decries 'pragmatic' government, and is nostalgic of what was in days gone by 'an underlying value' or ideology, as one might say. Does this have a place in business? I think so. You will have to act pragmatically of course. Business is partly the implementation of a plan, and partly opportunism. But there probably should be some underlying value in the operation you work for that will look after the long term as long as people keep it in mind.

I did some work in Digital at the time it started to implode, and that was what the people I was working with seemed to have lost. Their corporate sense of purpose was missing. We have already looked at Marks and Spencer in the same way. So make sure you have such a value behind your pragmatism, then go for the jugular.

John A. Hart (Group Personnel Director, PowerGen)

Career clue from the boardroom

In building a career, I have always thought it important that one should fulfil one's present job to the best of one's ability and, if one does well, promotion is likely to flow naturally, although I appreciate that this is not always the case.

Expressed in one line and accepting that it is something of a generality, my advice to young people would be 'set your sights high but climb the stairs one at a time.'

Sir David Lees (Chairman, GKN)

Idea 82 – Keep your plan flexible

Career clue from the Boardroom

- Aim high and achieve this by moving upwards between well-regarded organisations every two years.
- Work on continual self-improvement, courses, private study, new qualifications, professional memberships, extra work projects, etc.
- Be completely flexible on career moves that benefit. Relocate, move overseas, move to HQ and move again after a short period. Any career chance to progress up the ladder should be taken.
    P.R. Williams (Group Human Resources Director, Vodafone Airtouch)

The avalanche of advice to keep a flexible career plan continues. The career clue above echoes some previous ideas, but brings them together neatly.

Idea 83 – Make good decisions

Here is a technique you can use for making decisions that helps to balance the 'gut feel' of a decision with the logic behind it. You can use it if you are taking the decision on your own, or if you are involving a team and looking for consensus. Remember that, however senior you have become, you still normally have to take a team with you. I will describe it and its benefits in the case of a team decision.

It is useful to get the team used to using the same process each time they make an important decision. They will become more skilled in the process and get the maximum value out of the benefits of the process. These benefits include:

- *Faster decision-making*
  Since everyone knows the process, they will quickly eliminate some options and come to the alternative that makes most sense.
- *Better-quality decisions*
  You are aiming to make the right decision. Using a process removes some of the guesswork and means that the team's instincts and experience are most likely to come to the best choice.
- *Team consensus*
  Some team members may find that the decision made is not their first choice. If the team has used a logical process to make it, those who were against it to begin with are much more likely to be comfortable with the decision in the end.

Defining the ideal

First of all get the team to agree on the criteria against which they wish to measure the decision and the ideal performance against each criterion. Suppose, for example, they are looking at two options for a supplier of services. Ask them to brainstorm what an ideal solution would look like. Ask the questions, 'What do we want this solution to do for us?', and 'What benefits should we look for?' Make a list of these criteria. If you use a flip chart for the list, everybody will be using exactly the same words to describe the ideal. This list then gives the team a way of filtering options and comparing the alternatives. Your preparation for this exercise needs to be good, as the team will not necessarily have your personal career interests as one of the criteria.

Evaluating options

Agree with the team which of the criteria they should agree as most important. You

---

Career clue from the boardroom

Think carefully how you can make your boss's life easier. There is always a risk that your boss may rely upon you so much that he or she is reluctant to recommend you for promotion, but that is a risk worth taking in the quest to raise your profile in your boss's estimate.

George Paul (Chairman, Norwich Union)

---

may find that three or four stand out as vital. Now measure each of the options against the ideal agreed for each of these criteria. The process is logical, but still needs good creative thinking to evaluate the options. You may very well find that the decision is obvious after the evaluation against the main criteria. If not, take the next most important criterion and repeat the exercise. Keep going until one option stands out, or until the team is certain that, say, two options have nothing between them. Where that is the case, choose the option you think will be most acceptable to your superiors, since it will take less selling than the other one.

Validating decisions

You should also look at the downside – what would be the impact if we have made a wrong decision? If it would be catastrophic, you may want to think again and find a less risky route. Once again the risk is not only in terms of the organisation, but also in terms of your career. Finally use the acronym SAFE to validate the choice. SAFE stands for:

*   *Suitable*
    Is the decision the most suitable given the current situation?

- *Acceptable*
  Is the decision acceptable to all the stakeholders with an interest in it?
- *Feasible*
  Will it be feasible to implement the solution chosen, given time and resource constraints?
- *Enduring*
  Will the solution endure into the long term?

The SAFE test is a quick and useful check for any decision, team or individual, and can as well be used to test for career impact as business impact.

Idea 84 – Can we take that as read?

Chairing and managing meetings is an art, and one that successful people are good at.

The key to chairing a meeting successfully, apart from your charisma and style, is good discipline. The first discipline is attendance. If a person is due to attend a meeting, they must arrive. Do not allow some unexpected condition to excuse a person from attending. Everyone will get better at saying 'no' to meetings if you enforce this rule. At least if they say 'no', you can discuss it and agree if they need to be there.

The second major discipline is timekeeping. Insist from the outset that meetings will start on time. If your meetings gain the reputation of always starting late, attendees will begin to come later and later so that they do not waste their time. Talk about this at the first meetings of new teams, and be prepared to be very hard on latecomers particularly at that first meeting.

The third major discipline is progress reporting. Everyone must get used to the fact that their reports are required before the meeting for team members to do their

Career clue from the boardroom

No fast-track career was built on long meetings.

Richard Humphreys (serial Chairman)

preparation. If a team member fails in any of these disciplines, talk to them outside the meeting and ask for their assurance that it will not happen again. If they persist, then use any means at your disposal, including being nasty in front of their colleagues, to change the person's behaviour. The last discipline is on you. Are you sure that the meetings are objective-oriented and worthwhile, and that everyone you are asking to attend needs to be there?

*T*en *G*reatest *I*deas for *W*inning at *O*ffice *P*olitics

Introduction

In the early stages of the book we looked at people's machinations that we call company politics. Let's get a bit more personal now, and look at office politics. How do you make sure that how you behave and how you interact in the office is working in favour of your career rather than vice versa? When do you blow the whistle *Idea 88*? Why do you choose to work for the one person that everyone else avoids *Idea 91*? But we start with the somewhat depressing view of the great and the good about marrying the right person.

Idea 85 – Have the right corporate spouse

Evidently business leaders still believe that the spouse of their high fliers is an important accessory. I say spouse, but the magazine *Management Today* in its article on the topic majors almost entirely on male executives and their wives. Sir Bob Reid, the deputy governor of the Bank of England is reported to believe that having serial wives, say three, shows a lack of judgement. Not only that, but many recruiters believe that an executive is best served in career terms if his wife stays at home.

Their behaviour during company events is seen as important, from avoiding being the one who dances provocatively on the table at the Christmas party when young, to knowing that Japanese businessmen do not discuss business if their wives are with them, when the breadwinner has gone up a few levels. Ah well, *plus ça change.*

Career clue form the boardroom

Prioritise business and family life. Business is for a maximum of 40 years; family is for life.

Peter G. Birch (Chairman, Land Securities)

Idea 86 – Keep off the desk

It has been proved over the years unwise, if you are an attached person, to dally at work. Sex in the office is therefore a no-no to the careerist. Senior managers, particularly those who know and deal with your spouse, can hold it against you and, if it all becomes emotional, it can affect your performance at work – distracted, finding more and more obvious excuses for coming back late from lunch, talking to the pot plants and so on. Add in the jealousies that arise from the suspicion of favouritism, there need be no substance, and the case against sex is well made.

Having said that, even to the most red-in-tooth ambitious, some things are more important than the key to the executive washroom. Go for your life, you can always abscond to the competition.

Idea 87 – FIFO management

Make sure that you are sensitive to the culture of an organisation you are about to join. If it is a culture that expects its executives to work from eight in the morning to ten at night, do not expect to be able to win without taking your part in this mode of working. If the culture does not include your children's birthday as an excuse for not travelling to Argentina without notice, be aware that you will not be able to change that. Discuss it with your family and if they agree that such a life is worth the candle, then go for it. If you cannot convince them, then decide between them. (One woman high flier explained her decision to choose her career in these circumstances by saying, 'Good jobs are hard to come by, men are ten a penny.') If you cannot convince yourself, then look for an organisation that works differently. Gravitate towards an organisation that suits your choice in lifestyle.

Many junior managers think that FIFO management comes from an inventory-holding technique meaning *first in first out*. It doesn't; it stands for *fit in or fuck off*.

Idea 88 – Don't let anyone else blow the whistle

When it really goes pear shaped, it is very difficult to avoid the reputation that goes with being aboard a sinking ship. If this is the case, make sure that you are the whistle-blower and have compelling evidence that your superiors held you back by blocking your excellent decisions. If you tell the world this, or at least the trade press, then you may find the way ahead is in a more senior role with a competitor.

Idea 89 – Help the pressed

The trade press, and indeed the national press, is always looking for stories. They have a lot of white space to fill regularly. Feed them what you can. Study the trade press and get to know the journalists. Eventually they will start to ask you for comments on stories they have got from an alternative source. This gives you a profile outside your organisation and is good for improving your *gravitas*. Journalists are like the bees in the orchard flitting from source to source, they will help you to know where good people are, if that is what you are looking for, and also where good jobs are likely to be.

Idea 90 – If you live by the sword, don't blame the executioner

There is little more exciting in the executive's life than to be offered the chance to succeed where others have plainly failed. The board, or whoever, invites you to take over a sinking ship and 'turn it around'. Sometimes this is not as difficult as you may think. If the problem of the last incumbent was the failure to take tough and unpopular decisions, then all you may have to do to start the ball rolling in the right direction is to do that. Other times it seems impossible to take actions that will satisfy the board in terms of saving what they thought was saveable. This is called 'accepting a poisoned chalice', and is a well-known method used by senior managers to stuff the careers of people who are looking too hopeful of getting a top job at their expense.

Idea 91 – Go and work for that s***

There are always opportunities where there are problems. If a manager has a repu-

---

Career case in point

The outgoing manager of a basket case division of a large company gave no advice to the much younger person brought in to sort out the problems. He merely gave him three envelopes and an instruction to open them in order when the going seemed intractably tough.

After three months of frenzied activity, the young Turk had made no progress. All the figures were still aiming south and the morale problem if anything had worsened. Thinking that he had tried everything else, he opened the first envelope. It said, 'Be more vociferous in blaming your predecessor.' He published vicious papers and statistics showing 'just some' of the problems created and hidden by the people before him. It took the heat off for a while, but after a further three months the turning point seemed no nearer. He opened the second envelope. 'Re-organise one more time, this time substantially.' The newcomer threw the entire organisation up in the air and left no job unturned. He altered teams, roles and a number of business processes, still in the end to no effect. Discouraged and depressed, he opened the last envelope. It said 'Take three envelopes ...'

Career case in point

I once worked for a fiery project manager who walked roughshod over anyone he believed was endangering his project. He had a fine line in abuse, and never held back from using it, not only by telephone but also, more dangerously, in writing. I developed a good relationship with him and, with or without his agreement, toned down a lot of what he fired in his loose canon way around the company. I also worked hard on my relationship with his boss's secretary and she and I spoke often about smoothing off the rough edges of his direct approach. Between us we held the fort for about a year, until even we were powerless against a particularly vitriolic attack on a manager who was supporting an idea that happened to be the brainchild of the managing director. He left, and I, modestly, accepted the congratulations of his boss for having kept the man's talented contribution going for so long.

---

tation for being hard to work for and is generally unpopular, joining him or her may be exactly the right thing to do. There are a number of possible outcomes:

- If he or she is successful, then you should be able to paint yourself as the person who calmed the troubled waters and made success possible.
- If he or she is unsuccessful, everyone will understand that it was not your fault, and you will be left in charge when they leave.
- If the two of you fall apart, you may just be able to get some brownie points for trying.

Idea 92 – Smile, damn you, smile

It is official; people who can maintain positive facial expressions and body language do better than those who adopt a pose of the brusque and unsmilingly professional. Interviewers, for example, are notoriously bad at working out real personality; if you come across as sociable, outgoing, ambitious (but perhaps a bit of an animal lover on the side), this is who they will believe you to be. Intelligence also can be 'performed' to an extent; it has been proved that a candidate wearing glasses is generally considered to be more intelligent than one without.

On the intelligence stakes as well, there is the rather shocking truth that managers and interviewers regularly confuse how well you talk and the level of your language with your intelligence. Tone down that street talk and try to sound your 'th's; it all appears to count.

Career clue from the boardroom

Always show enthusiasm; never be intense.

Sir Roger Hurn (Chairman, Marconi)

Body language was big news a few years ago. Although we hear less about it now, the way you sit, stand, and what you do with your hands are integral to making an impression on a senior manager. Slow, relaxed movements are favoured. Remember to look like you are listening (you can listen, leaning back in your chair with your arms folded; but the key is, to let the interviewer realise that you are listening). Lean forward when being spoken to, back when speaking and nod your head to show that you are paying attention. Body language tends to work subconsciously; so be subtle in your movements. You do not want to look like a passenger on the top deck of a bus with St Vitus's dance. Finally, in regards to body language, if you remember nothing else, remember this: smile!

Of course, you could be a person who objects to having to alter your appearance, behaviour, language, in order to impress people with influence over your career. Surely they should accept you just as you are and do away with this arbitrary, classist nonsense? You are absolutely right. And whilst you sit smugly, secure in your political correctness, you can watch colleagues who are prepared to compromise and tow the line on the lesser details, advance their careers and fulfil their ambitions.

Idea 93 – Learn to love your human resources department

There was a time when a lot of line managers thought the personnel department an unnecessary luxury, allowing managers to skive off learning and applying company policies on staff. Indeed, Robert Townsend's advice of some years ago was to fire the entire department. But the days when the personnel department was looked down upon as a second-rate career are long gone. The department of human resources has grown up into a fully-fledged, respected and qualified unit. Human resource managers are masters of their trade.

When you are in charge of staff, you would be well advised to give due respect to the human resources department, as they could save you a lot of time, money and upset amongst your team.

The name of the game in terms of recruitment, staff monitoring and staff dismissal, is protecting the company. Laws regarding employer's liability, unfair dismissal and employment discrimination are tight. An unfair dismissal claim that goes the wrong way for an organisation could well send it into liquidation, as fines are high and are set to rocket even higher in the future, and the legal fees are extortionate.

A personnel department is definitely not something to skimp on. If your organisation is too small for a separate department, make sure that the person in charge of hiring and firing is adequately trained. A small outlay cost now could literally save you a fortune in the future.

In terms of your career, have as much to do with them as you can. Be the visiting speaker at training events and volunteer to be the pilot department for a new scheme, like replacement planning. They get used to a slightly sneering reception from many managers, until they need them that is, so take your usual contrarian approach and show them you love them.

Idea 94 – Get high at home

We started this section with sex, so we'll finish it with drink. As a manager, it is important to drop in at the pub where your people go, from time to time. Your job is not to be 'one of the boys', however, so don't get pissed. Your job is to be completely accepted by the group, but without becoming part of it. Do your serious drinking with your friends and family.

*T*hree *G*reatest *I*deas for *S*urviving *P*olitics

Introduction

We are talking *Politics* here with a capital P. Both at the top, *get your own PR Idea 95,* and further down the organisation, Politics will creep into your working life. Unless you are intent on becoming a Politician, as opposed to a politician, which you undoubtedly are already, the Vicar of Bray model looks not bad. If you finish your career with your closest colleagues still unaware of how you vote, you have probably played it as safe as possible.

Idea 95 – Get your own PR

At the top of the organisation you will have access to the company's PR advisers and internal team. By all means use it, but remember what their objectives are and to whom they report. It is just possible that your advancement might not even be on their agenda – bastards. By this time you probably need your own PR. So hire it. If you want a role model, try Charles Saatchi. Whenever you see him getting a lot of publicity, it is often not a company plug at all; so its source is probably not the company PR firm.

Idea 96 – It's sensitivity, not conviction

If your boss is an ardent SDLP supporter, it is inadvisable simply to join the SDLP. After all, your next one may be to the right of Ghengis Khan. Rather, you should fit in with them, and act sensitively. Obviously you avoid a flaming row, and this is probably true of everyone else as well. If their politics lean towards racism and discrimination, you may have to point out that what is being said is possibly illegal, and offer to explain the HR rules on such matters. Generally speaking, however, avoid such issues unless your political trigger makes an honest reaction more important than your career. Mmm. Political instincts in the pub are for one night, jobs are for profit and advancement.

Idea 97 – Understand your quarry

Try to get to know the politics of those around you. This enables you to avoid coming a cropper, and also tells you a lot about them. Listen to their political conversations; it helps you subsequently to know what to say to get your own way.

*T*hree *G*reatest *I*deas for *E*njoying the *L*ast *R*ung

Introduction

A career is for life, not just your working life. Before you leave the top job that reading this book has made almost inevitable, you still have your retirement to plan. Obviously you will have arranged the normal pre-retirement global business trip to pass on your final words of wisdom to the far-flung parts of the corporation. You will be taking your spouse, of course, since it lasts a long time. (I wonder if you know that people who do not make it to your dizzy heights call this a 'round-the-world retirement holiday' and – wait for it – pay for it themselves.)

But you are an active person and you need some stimulation to keep the grey cells busy. Here are the three greatest ideas.

Idea 98 – Line up the non-execs

Retirement, whether early or in your sixties, seems a bit dull if you have been in the hurly burly for a while. You need some non-executive directorships as an antidote to ennui, and an alternative to golf or the grandchildren. After all, to get to this stage in your career you must, at least at some point, have been interested in businesses and organisations.

Make sure you have lined these up before you retire. This is where the relationships you have with organisations apart from the ones you own can come in very useful. Suppliers come to mind. Henry Lewis, at one time chief executive of Marks and Spencer, was offered non-execs by a lot of his suppliers. One of them was so keen, indeed, that they kept back a sizeable chunk of shares so that they could offer them to Henry when he retired, in exchange for his coming on board as a non-exec.

It's a good life. You are paid a modest sum of money a year for preparing for and attending a board meeting every month. If asked, you can always take on a one-off project on behalf of the board, to keep your hand in. And if it gets a little niffy or unpleasant, like the grandchildren you simply hand the problem back to the people who own it and just – walk away.

Idea 99 – Form a government in exile

Another interesting and enjoyable pastime for the years of retirement after a long and successful career is to duplicate the board of the company you last worked for. It goes like this. You will have brought along and up the organisation a number of executives. These people will regard you as their mentor and you will regard them as your protégés. Once you have left, they will still want your advice and company, and you will still want the illusion of power. Easy. Just like the monthly board meeting organise a monthly meeting of the government in exile. Go out to lunch with your protégés and bitch the hell out of the new management. It is the final accolade – it was all right when you left it.

Idea 100 – Make sure that failure pays off handsomely

Klaus Esser, the last Chairman of Mannesman, advised his shareholders strongly to reject the hostile takeover bid from Vodafone Airtouch. In the end, the shareholders decided instead to reject his advice. So, does Herr Esser disappear into the sunset with a hangdog expression and three months' wages? Not a bit of it: according to *The Times*, he receives a 'golden goodbye' worth £19 million, of which 'more than half was agreed on the day the German company capitulated'. Mmm.

It is almost inevitable, strange as it may seem, for the chairman of any public enterprise eventually to fail. Either he or she will preside over a major cock-up, e.g. Marks and Spencer, or his or her shareholders will decide that someone else will make a better job of running the company, e.g. Mannesman. So the last greatest idea is to pre-empt this. Use your own lawyers, at the company's expense, to draw up your contract with failure heavily in mind. Get the security of share options and bonuses round you. You should certainly ally bonuses to performance measures but, in the small print, also make sure that they are paid independent of whether the performance measures are attained.

The total leaving package, again according to the *Times*, for Klaus Esser amounted to 43 times his annual salary at leaving, of £470,000. If you have stayed with the same company for all your working life, this settlement is the equivalent of being paid the same salary from year one, and when you leave the company being given your entire 43 years' earnings over again. Nice one, Klaus.

List of Contributors

Amanda Lebentz
Andy Bruce
Chris Wathen
Sir David Lees
G.W. Paul
Sir George Bull
Gordon M.W. Owen CBE
Graham McKenzie-Washington
Sir John Collins
John A. Hart
John Wright
Mark Allin
Lord Marshall of Knightsbridge
Murray Stuart CBE
P.R. Williams
Penny Ariff
Peter G. Birch
Sir Peter Walters
Richard Burton
Richard Humphreys
Sir Roger Hurn
Ros Jay

*P*ublications *C*onsulted

Anthony Jay and Ros Jay (2000) *Effective Presentation*, Prentice Hall, London.

Judith Johnstone, *Passing that Interview*, How To Books.

Jeff Davidson (1999) *The Complete Idiot's Guide to Managing your Time*, Alpha Books.

Brian Watling (1995) *The Appraisal Checklist*, Pitman.

Gavin Kennedy, John Benson and John McMillan (1980) *Managing Negotiations*, Business Books Ltd.